Physical Characteristics of the Dogue de Bordeaux

(from the FCI breed standard)

Neck: Very strong, muscular, almost cylindrical. Enormous neck with ample skin, loose and supple. Average circumference equals almost that of the head. The dewlap, well defined, starts at the level of the throat and forms folds to the chest.

Tail: Very thick at the base. The tip does not reach below the hock. Carried low, deeply set.

Hindquarters: Thighs are well developed and thick, muscles visible. Stifle in parallel plane to the vertical median plane or slightly turned inward or outward. Lower thigh is relatively short, muscular and well let down. Hock is short and sinewy with the angle of the hock relatively open.

Body: Chest is powerful, well ribbed up, broad, let down deeper than the elbows. Powerful forechest.

Coat: Fine hair which is short and soft to the touch.

Color: Solid color of mahogany (reddish brown) or in the range of the fawn shades. Good pigmentation is desirable. Small white patches on the chest and feet are allowed.

Size: Dogs at least 50 kg; for bitches at least 45 kg. Males: 60-68 cm at the withers; bitches 58-66 cm at the withers.

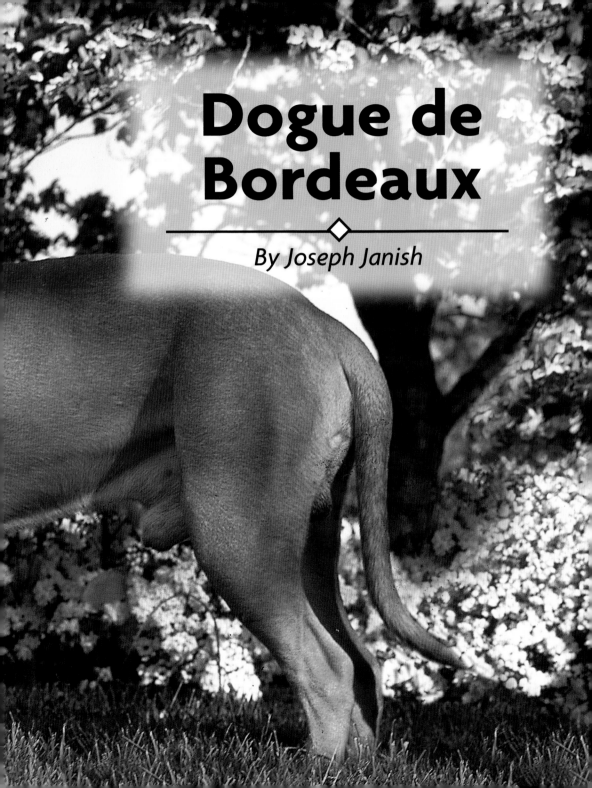

Dogue de Bordeaux

◇

By Joseph Janish

Contents

Training Your Dogue de Bordeaux   **88**

By Charlotte Schwartz
Be informed about the importance of training your Dogue de Bordeaux from the basics of housebreaking and understanding the development of a young dog to executing obedience commands (sit, stay, down, etc.).

Health Care of Your Dogue de Bordeaux   **113**

Discover how to select a qualified veterinarian and care for your dog at all stages of life. Topics include vaccination scheduling, skin problems, dealing with external and internal parasites and common medical and behavioral conditions.

Your Senior Dogue de Bordeaux   **144**

Recognize the signs of an aging dog, both behavioral and medical; implement a senior-care program with your veterinarian and become comfortable with making the final decisions and arrangements for your senior Dogue de Bordeaux.

Showing Your Dogue de Bordeaux   **151**

Experience the dog show world, including different types of shows and the making of a champion. Meet the Fédération Cynologique Internationale (FCI), the "world kennel club."

KENNEL CLUB BOOKS® **DOGUE DE BORDEAUX**
ISBN 13: 987-1-59378-215-3

Copyright © 2003, **2009** • Kennel Club Books® A Division of BowTie, Inc.
40 Broad Street, Freehold, NJ 07728 USA
Cover Design Patented: US 6,435,559 B2 • Printed in South Korea

10 9 8 7 6

Photo Credits:

Norvia Behling, Carolina Biological Supply, Doskocil, Fleabusters, Rx for Fleas, Isabelle Francais, Bane and Jeannie Harrison, James E. Hayden, RBP, James Hayden-Yoav, Carol Ann Johnson, Dwight R. Kuhn, Dr. Dennis Kunkel, Mikki Pet Products, Jean Claude Revy, Dr. Andrew Spielman, Alice van Kempen and C. James Webb

Illustrations by Renée Low.

HISTORY OF THE
Dogue de Bordeaux

INTRODUCTION

Characterized by one of the largest, most magnificent heads in dogdom, layered wrinkles on his face and hefty exaggerated paws, the Dogue de Bordeaux trudges into the hearts of people throughout the world. Originally used for cattle-droving and guarding the vineyards in Bordeaux, this pugnacious, pug-faced French warrior has survived within a hair of extinction through one national revolution, two World Wars and the Hollywood adventure *Turner and Hooch.*

Sometimes referred to as the French Mastiff, Bordeaux Bulldog or simply "DDB," the Dogue de Bordeaux has had an interesting background and development through the last six centuries. An extremely cooperative, intelligent and fearless giant, the Dogue de Bordeaux has persisted in various vocations throughout the centuries, a testament to the breed's versatility and adaptability. Since the 1400s, the Dogue de Bordeaux has had many jobs: herding cattle, flock guarding, hunting ferocious game, animal baiting, dog fighting and movie

Dogues de Bordeaux have a long history of being guard dogs. Their impressive stature alone is enough to frighten potential thieves.

Facing page: The Dogue de Bordeaux is often called the French Mastiff or Bordeaux Bulldog. One may recognize the Dogue as the star of the Hollywood production *Turner and Hooch,* with human co-star Tom Hanks.

GENUS CANIS

Dogs and wolves are members of the genus *Canis*. Wolves are known scientifically as *Canis lupus* while dogs are known as *Canis domesticus*. Dogs and wolves are known to interbreed. The term *canine* derives from the Latin-derived word *Canis*. The term *dog* has no scientific basis but has been used for thousands of years. The origin of the word *dog* has never been authoritatively ascertained.

acting. Powerful and surprisingly athletic, the Dogue de Bordeaux has never been intimidated and makes an excellent guardian. Beneath all that toughness exists a sweet, sincere, slobberingly lovable character that makes a wonderful companion.

HISTORY AND BACKGROUND OF THE DOGUE DE BORDEAUX

The Dogue de Bordeaux falls into a group of dogs classified as molossers, descendants of the Molossus, a dog that lived around the time of 700 BC. Based on ancient carvings and paintings, it appears that Molossus were kept as guard and hunting dogs by the Assyrians.

The first record of a molosser-type dog is in a letter dated 326 BC that mentions large, strong dogs with short, broad teeth. Bones of these big dogs have been found among other artifacts in archeological expeditions throughout the world in places such as Tibet, China and India. These dogs were included in the army of Alexander the Great, and journeyed from Mesopotamia to Epirus in various wars. In Epirus, there was a mythical king ruling over the area of Molossus who took care of the dogs. From there, they journeyed to Rome, Gaul and other lands, including Spain and France.

There are contrasting reports that this large dog first existed in Spain as the Alano, an extinct dog whose description resembles today's Dogue de Bordeaux. The Alano was supposedly brought to Europe by the Alans, an Oriental tribe. The *Alan vautre* was described in the 14th century by Gaston Phoebus (or Febus), Count of Foix, in his *Livre de Chasse*: "He holds his bite stronger than three sight hounds." There are also accounts that the molosser developed from the Molossid, a Greco-Roman canine that existed during Julius Caesar's time and was used in war.

DEVELOPMENT OF A DOGUE TYPE

The word *dogue* first appeared at the end of the 14th century. Before the 19th century, these dogs did not have a standard but were very similar in looks and usage. There were guardian dogs used to protect homes, butcher

The Tibetan Mastiff joins the Dogue de Bordeaux in the group of dogs known as molossers. Tibetans have curved tails and long coats, in contrast to the hanging tails and short coats of Dogues.

BRAIN AND BRAWN

Since dogs have been inbred for centuries, their physical and mental characteristics are constantly being changed to suit man's desires for hunting, retrieving, scenting, guarding and warming their masters' laps. During the past 150 years, dogs have been judged according to physical characteristics as well as functional abilities. Few breeds can boast a genuine balance between physique, working ability and temperament.

Tibetan Mastiff with puppy. Despite the shared ancestry, there is little resemblance to the Dogue.

shops and vineyards; pack hunting dogs that baited bulls and pursued boars, bears, jaguars and other game; and herding dogs that took care of farm animals such as sheep and cattle. Eventually, the molosser developed into a variety of mastiffs including today's Tibetan Mastiff, Spanish Mastiff, Mastino Napoletano (Neapolitan Mastiff) and Bullmastiff, to name a few.

One type of dog in France was called the Dogue or Doguin d'Aquitaine, a breed based on the French Molossus, which existed in the early 14th century and was bred for fighting other dogs, bears and boar. There were several variations of the Doguin d'Aquitaine, depending on their region and the jobs they needed to accomplish. As a result, their general appearance was inconsistent. There were various colors and varieties of coat, different jaw/bite patterns (undershot and overshot) and other slight variations. For the most part, however, these dogs were similar in body structure, weight and size. Eventually one type emerged as the preferred dog—the "butcher's dog" that was used to protect meat shops and was highly coveted by the French noblemen and wealthy families as home guardians.

The first recorded reference to "Dogue de Bordeaux" appeared in 1863 at the first canine exhibition at the Jardin d'Acclimatation in Paris, France. This was less a conformation show than it was a

The incorporation of the Dogue de Bordeaux into the Japanese Fighting Dog resulted in today's Tosa Inu, shown here.

presentation of dog breeds. The winner of the exhibition was a bitch named Magentas who was identified according to the capital of her region of origin—thus, Dogue de Bordeaux.

Toward the end of the 19th century, the Dogue de Bordeaux traveled to England for fighting and show competition. In 1895, John Proctor published an article in the magazine *The Stock Keeper* describing his experience judging the "fighting dogs of the South of France." When English law made dog fighting illegal, the Dogue de Bordeaux was bred almost exclusively for conformation and temperament for competition in dog shows.

In 1896, veterinarian Pierre Meguin published the standard for the Dogue de Bordeaux in his magazine *L'Eleveur* ("The Animal Breeder"). He formalized a standard from a combination of the best Dogues de Bordeaux shown since Magentas captured top-dog honors at the Jardin d'Acclimatation. This standard was put forward by Meguin with a Mr. Brooke, Dr. Wiart and a group of French authorities. A year later, the standard was published in *The Breeds of Dog* by Henry de Bylandt.

Until Meguin's standard, there was much controversy over Dogue type, and diversity in breed type persisted. Head and body size fluctuated according to the particular breeder, both scissors and undershot bites were found and the mask color was extremely varied. During this time of uncertainty, there were at least three different styles of Dogue: the Toulouse, the Paris and the Bordeaux. The Toulouse had a fawn coat or brindle coat of many colors, but otherwise was very similar to today's Dogue de Bordeaux. The Paris was also similar to the modern standard, but the bite varied, with some having a scissors bite while others were nearly one inch undershot. After much debate, the breeders decided upon the undershot bite found in today's Dogue de Bordeaux standard.

In 1910, after three years of research, J. Kunstler, a professor of comparative anatomy at the Science Facility of Bordeaux, wrote *Etude Critique du Dogue de Bordeaux*, a critical study of the breed that included a more precise standard than the original published by Meguin. Kunstler's standard is used to this

Front view of the Tosa Inu. The word *inu* in Japanese means "dog."

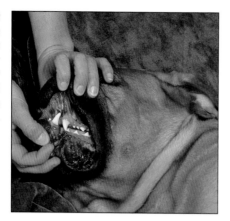

The undershot bite, where the lower jaw protrudes further than the upper jaw, is required according to the breed standard.

day (albeit updated twice by Dr. Raymond Triquet and Mr. Tim Taylor), though there are still some variations of the breed, identified as the Bordeaux type, the Paris type and the Mediterranean type. The differences between these types are slight and have mainly to do with the height and the head.

The breed standard evolved as interest in the Dogue de Bordeaux increased. The first standard (*Caractere des vrais dogues*) by Pierre Meguin appeared in *Le Dogue de Bordeaux* in 1896. The second standard was developed by J. Kunstler and appeared in *Etude critique du Dogue de Bordeaux* in 1910. The third standard was produced by breed expert Dr. Raymond Triquet, with the collaboration of Dr. Maurice, a veterinarian, in 1971. The fourth standard was reformulated according to the Fédération Cynologique Internationale's (FCI) Jerusalem model by Dr. Triquet,

with the collaboration of Philippe Serouil, President of the French Dogue de Bordeaux Club in 1993.

EXPORTATION OF THE DOGUE
After the standard became known throughout the world, it was only a matter of time before the Dogue de Bordeaux was in demand for breeding programs abroad. During the 1930s, the impressive size and character of the Dogue de Bordeaux attracted others to incorporate the breed into the Japanese Fighting Dog. Increasing the head and overall body size of Japan's Fighting Dog resulted in today's Tosa Inu. Similarly, the Martinez brothers of Argentina imported several Dogues de Bordeaux for infusion into their breeding program. Their goal was a super dog that needed the Dogue's head size, overall size and strength, jaw strength and courage. These same characteristics are essential elements of today's Dogo Argentino, the solid white creation of the Martinez brothers designed to pursue large game.

In the 1960s, Dr. Philip Todd imported the Dogue de Bordeaux into the US, then moved with his Dogues to Holland and introduced the breed to the Dutch. Toward the end of the 1960s, Dr. Todd helped Steve and Wendy Norris establish a breeding program in the US.

Throughout the world, the

The English Mastiff is another molosser cousin of the Dogue de Bordeaux.

Dogue de Bordeaux is recognized by canine organizations; the FCI, The Kennel Club (UK), the United Kennel Club (US) and the American Rare Breed Association (US) are among the most notable registries. The American Kennel Club (AKC), the largest canine registry in the US, still does not recognize the breed.

DOGUES AROUND THE WORLD

In the 1800s, the breed was hardly known outside his native France, although some exports to England took place as early as

The Boxer and the Dogue resemble each other in certain facial features.

1885 for the purpose of fighting and later for conformation shows. The first breeder of the Dogue in Scandinavia was H. Kröller from Aalborg in Denmark in the beginning of the 20th century.

THE UNITED STATES

Introduced to the US in the 1960s by Dr. Philip Todd and later campaigned by the hard-working Steve and Wendy Norris, the Dogue de Bordeaux found good friends in the US. The American dog world, however, had not grasped on to this quintessential French mastiff and, for the first 20 years, very few Dogues existed in the US and few, if any, serious fanciers committed themselves to the breed. By the 1980s, the Dogue de Bordeaux Club of America, dedicated to improving and importing quality specimens from Europe, made a great impact on the breed in America. The new parent club became well established with French breeders and experts, and only the finest Dogues made their way to America. More and more dog fanciers noticed the Dogue, and considerable interest was developing in the breed.

In 1989, the breed gained in popularity after the release of the movie *Turner and Hooch*, starring Tom Hanks and featuring a well-trained, entertaining and attractive Dogue de Bordeaux. As the movie gained popularity, so did the breed—a double-edged sword for the Dogue de Bordeaux. It was good that North Americans were finally learning about this magnificent breed, but this surge in popularity was unfortunately a bane for the breed. Too many profit-motivated, incompetent breeders quickly bred Dogues de Bordeaux that were not sound and did not conform to type. They bred Dogues with hip dysplasia or other known genetic maladies. Inbreeding was common and resulted in many Dogues with poor temperament and behavioral problems.

From the 1990s on, responsible Dogue de Bordeaux breeders have kept the proper Dogue type intact. The Dogue de Bordeaux Society has done an outstanding job of preserving type, and has established a rescue organization that places stray or abandoned Dogues de Bordeaux in adoptive homes that adhere to the organization's code of ethics. The rescue organization also will assist Dogue de Bordeaux owners who, for any reason, can no longer provide a home for their dog.

The United States Bordeaux Corporation is a similar organization with a specific code of ethics and the goal of betterment for the breed. These clubs, along with registries such as the American

The Neapolitan Mastiff has a heavier head than the Dogue, yet it is still quite evident that the two breeds are related.

Rare Breed Association (ARBA) and the United Kennel Club (UKC), sponsor shows and events that welcome the Dogue de Bordeaux.

By and by, the Dogue de Bordeaux has a long way to go to become a popular pet or a household name. In the US, the breed is still regarded as a "rare breed." Although a dog show for rare breeds may attract as many as 25 quality Dogues de Bordeaux, this display in no way indicates that the breed is becoming as popular as the Great Dane or Bullmastiff, for example. Fortunately, there are many devoted breeders who will continue to promote the breed and

Nothing is as impressive as the head of the Dogue de Bordeaux, the grandest head in the dog world.

establish an enthusiastic following in the United States.

THE UNITED KINGDOM

After five years of advocacy by the British Dogue de Bordeaux Club, The Kennel Club of Britain finally accepted the Dogue de Bordeaux in November of 1998. This move by The Kennel Club came just a few months after Dr. Raymond Triquet, known to many as the "Father of the Dogue de Bordeaux," spoke at a seminar in Ascot, England. His presentation championing the breed was a key element in persuading The Kennel Club toward acceptance. The introduction of the breed was celebrated at a special exhibition of several Dogues de Bordeaux at Earls Court, the venue of the original Crufts Dog Show. Credit should also go to the most influential and supportive members of the British Dogue de Bordeaux Club, including Ann Sutton, Karen Watson, Alan and Kerry Bates and Paul and Karen Harris.

GERMANY

The Dogue de Bordeaux was introduced into Germany in the mid to late 1800s for many of the same reasons that the breed found popularity in France. In Germany, the Dogue de Bordeaux was a valuable working dog on farms, droving cattle and guarding flocks. Unrivaled as a protector and hunter, it was also used for hunting game and preventing wild boars from dismantling vineyards, farmlands and stock animals.

In 1908, a breed club was established for the Dogue de Bordeaux, the Allgemeiner Deutscher Bordeauxdoggen. After World War II, this breed club was one of the founding members of the Verband fuer das Deutsche Hundewesen (VDH). Until 1978, this club was known under the name Club fuer Bordeauxdoggen und Mastiffs e.V. When the Neapolitan Mastiff, Bullmastiff, Fila Brasileiro, Tosa Inu and Spanish Mastiff joined the organization, it was renamed Club fuer Molosser e.V. (Club for Molossian Breeds).

The breeds are under the supervision of several working groups (Arbeitsgemeinschaften = AG). Each breed has its own working group, with one president who is elected by the group for two years.

SPAIN

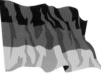

Currently there are a few small bands of breeders who are developing excellent examples of the breed, and the Dogue is

Although the Dogue de Bordeaux should not look like an "overgrown Bulldog," there are evident similarities between the English Bulldog, shown here, and the Dogue. Inset: A head study of the English Bulldog.

gaining popularity throughout the country. The breed has no specific national organization but is recognized by the Club Español de los Molosos de Arena, a club for Molosser-type dogs that is similar to the German Club fuer Molosser e.V. Both the FCI and the Real Sociedad Canina sanction this club.

ITALY

The Dogue de Bordeaux is beginning to enjoy popularity throughout Italy. It has benefited from the Club Italiano del Molosso (CIM), an organization whose mission is to encourage, promote and educate breeders to preserve a superior strain in each of the following breeds: Bullmastiff, Dogue de Bordeaux, Dogo Argentino, Fila Brasileiro, Spanish Mastiff, Tibetan Mastiff, Pyrenean Mastiff and Tosa Inu. Their goal is to strengthen the selection of the Molossian breeds identified by the second group of the Italian Kennel Club (ENCI) that are not specifically represented or protected by another breeders' association.

CIM is an excellent organization that publishes an informative newsletter (*I nostri cani*) and a quarterly bulletin. It also organizes shows under the authority of, and in collaboration with, ENCI. CIM membership is open to Italian citizens as well as foreigners who agree to abide by the statutes, and whose application is accepted by the council. Those interested in finding out more about the Dogue de Bordeaux in Italy should contact ENCI in Milan or CIM in Felino (Parma).

NETHERLANDS

In July 1975, the first litter of Dogues de Bordeaux was born in the Netherlands at the kennel of Mr. Van den Doel in Berg en Dal. The only thing known about this litter is its NHSB (the Netherlands Dog Registry) registration.

Four years later, the second litter was born, an "A-litter" of Dogues de Bordeaux "Van de Ircomara," at the kennel of Mrs. F. Schietekatte. The dam was a French import named Lia de Ker Saint Mesmes. The sire was Lex de la Berse du Loup from Germany. Development was slow and type inconsistent from there.

Dutch conformation shows have recently begun to include many Dogues de Bordeaux. The quality of the breed has improved drastically since the 1980s and, as a result, judging has been more consistent. Prior to the 1980s, judges were simply looking for the good type, a common tactic with new breeds. Now that the ring participants are conforming

There are clubs worldwide who are devoted to preserving type in molosser breeds such as the Dogo Argentino, shown here, and the Dogue de Bordeaux.

to the accepted standard, judges can concentrate on the specifics such as finding the right balance between type and other qualities such as the body and the movement. Dutch breeders have succeeded fairly quickly in their objective of creating Dogues de Bordeaux with heavy bone, massive size, more wrinkles and fuller noses that compare favorably with the top Dogues in France. Judge Mr. Bas Bosch N'Agor, who spent most of the 1980s studying the breed in France, has had a strong influence on the positive development of the Dogue de Bordeaux in the Netherlands.

The Dogue played an active role in the creation of the Dogo Argentino.

Support for the argument that the Dutch can breed great Dogues de Bordeaux came in 1994 when the bitch Nike de Legeane, bred by J. Dijkstra and owned by Erik Planting, became World Champion. Also in 1994, the bitch Fitou Appelation Controlee, bred and owned by Erik Planting, was named Best Youth Bitch at the club match in Germany (UBX).

In 1996, the bitch Lady Boss de la Maison de Hollande, bred and owned by Gerard van't Hul, tallied two youth titles: Youth World Champion and Youth Luxembourg Champion, and also won at the club match in Italy. Other Dutch Dogue de Bordeaux victories took place at the National d'Elevage in France, where the male Mike, bred by F. van Tuyl, became Best Youth Male, Lady Boss de la Maison de Hollande became Best Youth Bitch and Arlet van de Amilja, bred by J. Bosma, became Best Bitch.

In spite of all these achievements, the Dutch continue to concentrate on preserving the athleticism, movement, personality and other qualities as well as keeping good type. The worst fear among breeders in the Netherlands is that the Dogue de Bordeaux will get too large, heavy and bulky—characteristics that are equally despised in the rest of the world.

Much of the Netherlands' success can be attributed to

A Dogue male with his puppy. These are Dutch-bred dogs.

Belmondo the Red Powerpack, a spectacular, dark red Dogue de Bordeaux that had great size and heavy bone yet retained the athleticism that is so desired in the breed. Belmondo was imported from Germany by Mrs. Antonissen-van Strien. He was big and possessed wonderful bone, a massive classic head with a perfect nose, a rare perfect topline and very strong forequarters and hindquarters. He was named "*Dog World*'s Top Dog of the Year 1992" in the Netherlands. His greatest foreign result was in 1994 when he gained Best of Breed at the World Dog Show in Switzerland under the "Father of the Dogue de Bordeaux," Dr. Raymond Triquet. Belmondo is credited with 18 litters between 1988 and 1997 that produced numerous champions. Before Belmondo, the most important Dogue was N'Agor de la Maison des Coqs x Lutteur du Gorge d'Or, who was the base of all breeding in Holland in the 1980s.

The Bullmastiff is a close relative of the Dogue. Inset: A head study of the Bullmastiff.

CHARACTERISTICS OF THE
Dogue de Bordeaux

PHYSICAL CHARACTERISTICS OF THE DOGUE DE BORDEAUX

The Dogue de Bordeaux is a powerful, muscular dog that makes an excellent guard of both person and property. A compact, strongly built athlete, the Dogue possesses size that belies his agility and speed. These qualities were originally developed for working, protecting property and hunting. As you study the Dogue's characteristics, keep in mind the breed's original purposes.

The jaws are prominent due to strong development of the chewing muscle. This was a necessary characteristic for bull-baiting. The chest is very broad and deep, let down below the elbows. Its depth is more than half the dog's height at the withers; this is regarded as an important proportion. The Dogue de Bordeaux should not look like an oversized Bulldog.

The coat is short, fine and silky, colored in all shades of red and fawn to deep red mahogany. Good pigmentation of skin is favored. White markings on the chest and feet are tolerated. The Dogue de Bordeaux should have a well-marked red or black facial mask. The color of the nose corresponds to that of the mask.

TEMPERAMENT

Like all molosser-type dogs, the Dogue de Bordeaux has strong nerves and is not easily excited. His personality is balanced, quiet and calm. Not very rowdy, it is rare to hear the Dogue de Bordeaux bark loudly without sufficient reason (i.e., an intruder entering the home). This is a very confident breed that does not need to prove itself to other dogs, unless it is challenged.

The Dogue de Bordeaux is a charming breed that is very warm and friendly to humans and small animals. It is a very good dog with children for two reasons. First, the Dogue de Bordeaux loves to be around humans—a family cannot be big enough. Second, the Dogue de Bordeaux has plenty of patience and will deal with the typical teasing, tail pulling and other annoyances in which exuberant children tend to engage. Dogues are happy to comply with the silliest of children's games, such as wearing hats and playing "dress-up."

The Dogue de Bordeaux is intelligent, docile and usually not inclined to fight. Male dogs tend to be more dominant and will occasionally fight with other

The impressive presence of a Dogue is a great deterrent to thieves. Despite his intimidating appearance, the Dogue is a charmer who loves to be with people, especially children. Inset: Make no mistake—the Dogue is a formidable guard dog with the brawn to stand up to his bark.

males to determine dominance. Dominance is an inherent trait of the Dogue de Bordeaux and must be accepted and dealt with by the Dogue owner.

Keep in mind that one of the original purposes of the Dogue de Bordeaux was to protect, which in many cases meant to fight. As a result, the Dogue de Bordeaux is dog-aggressive by nature, will not back down from a fight (though is unlikely to instigate one) and will protect what is his own (and his owners'). Proper socialization of your Dogue is of the highest importance, and even well-socialized Dogues de Bordeaux must be monitored when in the presence of other dogs.

The Dogue de Bordeaux tends to be a very stubborn and arrogant breed, yet it is very trainable. Once the Dogue learns a command, he will never forget it. Because of his high intelligence, it is necessary to continue beyond basic obedience training. If you will not be using your Dogue de Bordeaux for hunting, trials, Schutzhund or other competition, then engage him in special tasks and jobs around the home. You will be surprised at how much your Dogue can learn and help with your everyday routine, with the added benefit that your pet will never be bored.

When training your Dogue de Bordeaux, always keep in mind his self-confidence, arrogance, independence and stubborn nature. Thus, it makes no sense to scream, scold and shout like a drill sergeant. You will get much further by combining training with playtime—nothing is easier for a dog (and owner!) than learning by playing. You must use praise, rather than negativity, to train your Dogue de Bordeaux. Praise is the most important aid to education and will yield the quickest results. Praise everything your Dogue does correctly, from doing his duty outside to bringing in the newspaper.

Training your Dogue de Bordeaux requires patience, love and a well-filled bag of tricks to be successful. If the learning process is supported by pieces of meat, cheese or other delicacies, the Dogue de Bordeaux learns even more quickly. The smell of food has a magical way of eliminating the Dogue de Bordeaux's ego. Your most effective argument should be positive reinforcement—not physical clout. When necessary, the best reprimand is to shake the scruff of the neck.

Consistency is another essential element of successful training. If you cannot withstand your puppy's pleading look and allow him to sit on the sofa, then it will soon be his sofa, not yours! Letting the puppy sleep in bed and feeding him from the table are similar examples. Keep in mind that the cute pug-faced puppy snuggling beside you will very shortly become a huge, heavy, slobbering 100-lb dog that takes up the entire bed or sofa and will not be inclined to move from his comfortable spot.

THE DOGUE DE BORDEAUX IN THE HOME

A willing worker who is happy to be around people and fairly cooperative, the Dogue de Bordeaux makes a wonderful addition to a happy home. Dogues get along

The Dogue will have no trouble making himself at home. If you choose to allow your Dogue on the couch, make sure he leaves some room for you!

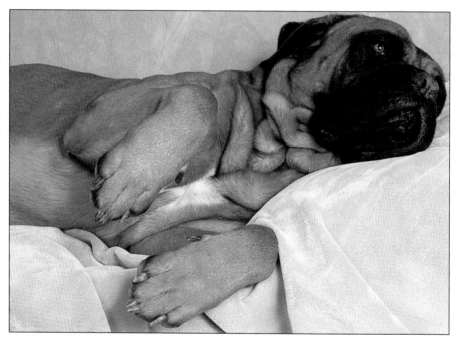

Many believe that the Dogue de Bordeaux's intelligence and independent personality make him unresponsive to repeated instructions. Do not be discouraged. Every year, many Dogues de Bordeaux successfully pass obedience exams and compete strongly in obedience trials. Practice patience, use rewards and be mentally stronger than your dog, and you will prevail.

with other family pets and, if introduced early, can make friends with cats, birds and other dogs—depending on the compatibility of the collective personalities. There could be problems with having two male dogs with dominant personalities, and it is generally recommended to have dogs of opposite sex sharing a home. If you must have two males in the home, try to keep the age

Allowing the Dogue de Bordeaux into your home is akin to giving this gentle giant the lease to your heart as well. This is an affectionate, amusing companion for the right family and home.

A bitch with two of her offspring. Even young puppies have serious, intelligent looks on their faces.

difference as great as possible. Few young puppies will try to challenge the authority of a full-grown male and they will be quick to learn under the older dog's guidance and stature.

All of this is also valid for bitches. In both cases, it is advisable to show the puppy to the "old" dog and observe the older dog's reactions. Do not force the puppy's integration if the older

ACTIVITY

During playtime, training or exercise, you should be aware of your puppy's condition. Puppies should be given rest when needed. This should not be difficult to ascertain since puppies are usually very anxious, inquisitive and full of energy. When the puppy seems tired, he definitely needs to relax. The growth of the puppy is so fast that the tendons and ligaments—as for all large breeds—have to endure a great strain. When taking the puppy for a walk, pace yourself. Increase the time/distance slowly during the first few months. A longer walk is possible after eight or nine months, but keep attuned to your puppy's condition. Remember that most of the growing process takes place during the first year. It shouldn't be a problem for a healthy adult Dogue de Bordeaux to go for a 5-mile walk, but not on a hot summer day.

The Dogue de Bordeaux loves to play and is always ready for fun, even in old age. Retrieving a frisbee or running after a ball may remind some Dogues de Bordeaux too much of work, but the same dog will be tireless while conquering an old towel or a potato sack.

Can a Dogue de Bordeaux run next to a bike? Yes and no. As long as you are not training for the Tour de France, it shouldn't be a problem for your full-grown Dogue. A calm, even-paced ride around the

Unlike many other giant mastiffs, the Dogue de Bordeaux is an active, athletic animal that revels in a game of fetch with his master.

dog shows a defensive or aggressive reaction. If the older dog does not accept the puppy, it might be best to reconsider the acquisition, otherwise you will live in a permanent state of conflict.

As with other pets, the Dogue de Bordeaux will get along with children if introduced early and properly. Generally, there will be no problem if the child was there before the puppy. Always make sure that the child isn't abusive to the dog; it can be quite tempting for a young toddler to tease a tolerant Dogue de Bordeaux. This may be hard to believe, but adult supervision is more necessary for the Dogue's safety than for the child's. By nature, the Dogue is docile and kindhearted and loves human affection. Any Dogue de Bordeaux that is aggressive to humans without being provoked is atypical of the breed.

park will be good, fun exercise for the both of you. As with walking, be sure to start off slowly and work your Dogue up to a pace that you both can handle.

HEALTH CONCERNS

The Dogue lives an average of eight to ten years. As for most other large-boned dogs, hip dysplasia is the most common problem in the breed. Good breeders have their Dogues de Bordeaux screened for hip dysplasia and exclude affected dogs from their breeding programs. Unfortunately, the rise in popularity of the breed has resulted in many incompetent breeders who have bred unsound, inferior Dogues with bad hips. Eliminating this condition is a constant battle.

You had better train your Dogue to heel, or else he will be dragging you on the other end of the leash.

In France at one time, the Dogue de Bordeaux was tested for hip dysplasia in the following manner, according to rare-dog expert Carl Semencic:

"At two years of age, any Dogue that displays the physical and temperamental characteristics required for possible use in a breeding program is made to jump a fence that stands three feet high. Any Dogue that cannot easily clear the fence is excluded from any breeding plans."

This may sound like a rather unscientific method of testing your Dogue, but it makes perfect sense. The Dogue de Bordeaux is supposed to be an athletically fit dog with powerful, muscular legs. Any Dogue that does not fit this description should not be considered for breeding.

Heart murmurs and skin diseases are also problems with the Dogue. Heart murmurs can be attributed to the small gene pool that composes our Dogues today. Demodectic mange is a skin problem rarely discussed among breeders, yet seems to be a problem for the Dogue de Bordeaux. This irritation is the result of a mite that lives on the dog and compromises the dog when the immune system is low. These mites feed faster than the body can reproduce cells, and they take over. Often this is mistaken for staph infection unless skin scrapings are done.

The Dogue de Bordeaux is a fast-growing dog. Puppies can gain 5 pounds a week on average and may experience eosinphilic panosteitis (also called "pano"), better known as "growing pains" or wandering lameness. Pano is an acute lameness unrelated to trauma. It shifts from one location to another and is accompanied by a fever.

Dogues de Bordeaux are also prone to bloat, a twisting of the stomach that could lead to death. Although the experts are not in agreement as to the exact causes, excessive exercise and excitement before or after eating and drinking can cause bloat. Bloat is most commonly traced to the dog's gulping air, which gets caught in the stomach. To prevent this, avoid feeding your Dogue de Bordeaux immediately before or after exercise, and feed several small portions throughout the day. Do not fill a huge dish with food and leave it there all day. Rather, keep feeding times consistent and remove the food bowl from the dog's reach when he has finished eating. Leave water available during the day, but not at feeding time. Many breeders recommend the use of a bowl stand to avoid the Dogue's craning his neck to reach his food bowls.

The Dogue needs a lot of exercise to develop his muscle structure. As with all large and heavy breeds, problems with tendons and ligaments can occur during the periods of quick growth. During these times, the Dogue de Bordeaux puppy should not be engaged in vigorous activities. Young pups get much of their exercise from regular play rather than from strenuous exercise, but as the Dogue gets older, it is very important that he receive the proper amount of exercise. Your Dogue de Bordeaux will get the exercise he needs if you include him in your daily routine and take him on special jaunts such as hikes, hunts, jogs, etc. You should walk your Dogue at least twice a day and try to find time for an extended run or playtime a few times a week.

Special note: The Dogue de Bordeaux is very sensitive to anesthesia. A "normal" dose can be lethal. Take extra special care in choosing a veterinarian who is familiar with the breed and its idiosyncrasies—it could save your Dogue de Bordeaux's life!

Do not offer your Dogue small toys or anything that can be swallowed easily. Only offer large, strong chew toys made especially for large dogs and powerful jaws.

Physical Structure of the Dogue de Bordeaux

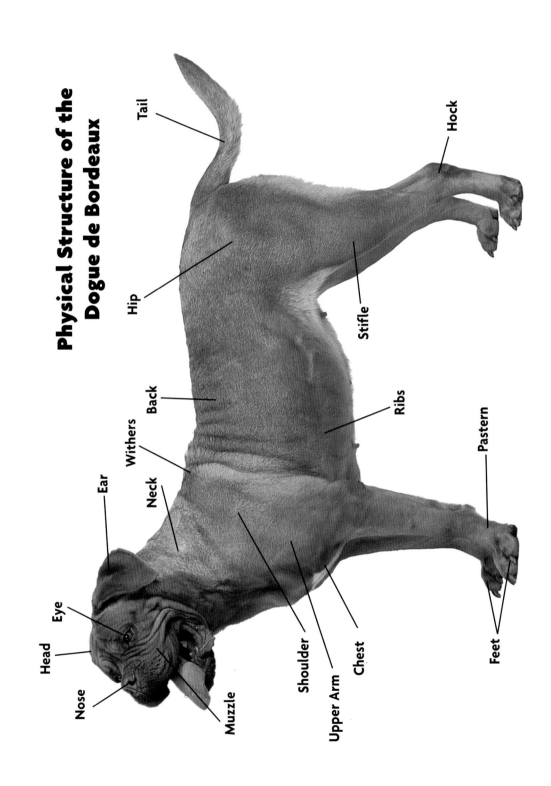

Tail

Hock

Hip

Stifle

Back

Withers

Ribs

Neck

Ear

Pastern

Eye

Head

Shoulder

Nose

Upper Arm

Chest

Muzzle

Feet

Dogue de Bordeaux

The standard, by which breeders breed and judges judge, is a written description of the perfect Dogue de Bordeaux. The current FCI standard, a few generations from the standard drafted by J. Kunstler, was devised by Raymond Triquet, breeder and judge of the Dogue de Bordeaux, recognized as the world authority. This "blueprint" of the perfect Dogue de Bordeaux is intended to assist the reader to envision what the ideal specimen of this breed should look like. While standards are subjected to the reader's interpretation, this word picture is the accepted means by which show people evaluate their dogs. If a dog does not match closely to the standard, it will neither be included in a breeding program nor campaigned as a show dog. Only the very best Dogues de Bordeaux should be bred in order to produce top-quality puppies in the next generation.

Pet owners should keep in mind that, although they may never intend to enter a dog show (or even attend one), the standard will help them to learn what is acceptable in a good specimen and what is not. Physically, the Dogue de Bordeaux is one of the most imposing, impressive and arguably beautiful of all dogs. Why settle for an untypical, unimpressive specimen? An educated approach to dog ownership is the best approach. The following description is based on the breed standard of the FCI.

THE BREED STANDARD FOR THE DOGUE DE BORDEAUX
Origin and Purpose: Originated from France. Used in ancient times as a fighting dog, and used today as a companion and guard dog.

General Appearance: The Bordeaux Mastiff is a massive, powerfully built dog, with a very muscular body that retains a harmonious general outline. In stature, somewhat low to the ground. Distance from sternum to ground is at most equal or inferior to the depth of the chest, seen in profile and measured behind the elbows. Has the appearance of an athlete, imposing and proud, demanding respect.

Temperament: Assumes guard with vigilance and great courage, but without aggressiveness. Very attached to the master and very affectionate with children.

Side view of a well-built Dogue de Bordeaux. This is an imposing figure: muscular, athletic and powerful.

The size of a Dogue's body should be in direct relation to the size of its head. Examples of (left) a well-proportioned head and (right) a head that is too small.

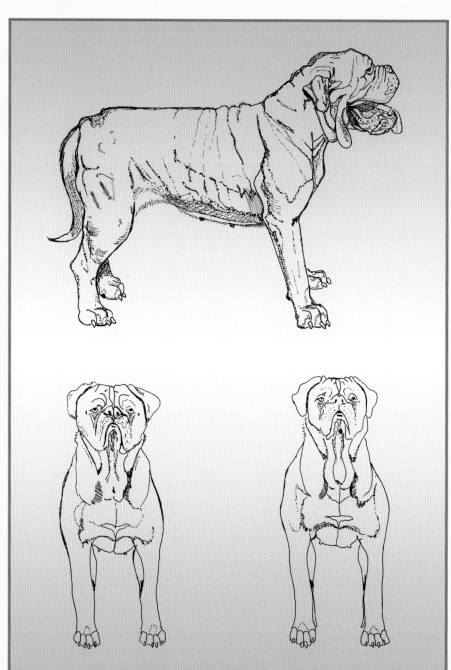

Size: Weight for dogs is at least 50 kg (110 lb); for bitches, at least 45 kg (99 lb). Size should more or less correspond to head measurement. Males: 60–68 cm (approx. 23.5–26.5 in) at the withers; bitches 58–66 cm (approx. 23–26 in) at the withers.

Coat and Color: *Color:* Solid color of mahogany (reddish brown), or in the range of the fawn shades. Good pigmentation is desirable. Small white patches on the chest and feet are allowed. *Coat:* Fine hair, short and soft to the touch.

Head: *Skull:* In the male, the perimeter of the skull measured at the level of its greatest width corresponds to the height at the withers. In the female, it may be slightly less. Its volume and its shape are the consequences of the very important development of the temporal, supraorbital ridges, zygomatic arches, and the spacing of the branches of the lower jaw. The upper region of the skull is slightly convex from side to side. Frontal-nasal depression of stop is very pronounced, almost at a right angle with the muzzle. The frontal groove is deep, diminishing toward the back of the head. The forehead dominates the face, yet is still wider than high.

Muzzle: Powerful, broad, thick, rather short, upper line very slightly concave, moderately obvious folds. Its width hardly decreases toward the end of the muzzle. When seen from above, it has the shape of a square. In relation to the upper region of the skull, the line of the muzzle forms an obtuse angle upwards. When head is held horizontally, the front end of the muzzle is blunt, thick and broad at the base, in front of a vertical tangent to the anterior face of the nose. Its perimeter is close to two-thirds of that of the head. Its length varies between a quarter and a third of the total length of the head, from the nose to the occipital crest.

Nose: Broad, well-opened nostrils, well pigmented black or brown according to the mask. Turned-up nose permitted.

Mouth: Jaws are very powerful and broad. Undershot bite. Lower jaw must project 0.5 cm (almost .2 in) minimum to 2 cm (almost .8 in) maximum. The incisors and canines must not be visible when mouth is closed. Teeth are very strong; strong canines; lower canines set wide apart and slightly curved. Incisors well aligned especially in lower jaw where they form an apparently straight line. Lips are thick, moderately pendulous, retractable, rounded over the lower jaw.

Eyes: Oval and set well apart. The space between the two inner

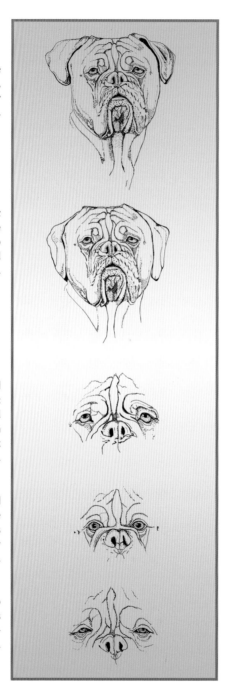

The ears should be high set and short, not falling too far below the eye.

These ears are set too low on the head and are too long, reaching well below the nose.

The preferred facial features: eyes set well apart, oval, with frank expression.

Eyes are too round and set too close together. Face is too narrow overall.

Eyes are too slanted; face lacks the desired expression.

angles of the eyelids equals about twice the length of the eye (eye opening). Frank expression. Hazel to dark brown for a dog with a black mask; lighter color tolerated but not desirable in subjects with a red mask.

Ears: Relatively small, of a slightly darker color than the coat. At its set on, the ear base is slightly raised in front but must fall back, without limpness along the cheeks. The tip is slightly rounded and must not reach much beyond the eye. Quite high set, at level of the upper line of the skull, the width of which they seem to accentuate even more.

Neck: Very strong, muscular, almost cylindrical. Enormous neck with ample skin, loose and supple. Average circumference equals almost that of the head. It is separated from the head by a slight transversal furrow, slightly curved. Its upper profile is slightly convex. The dewlap, well defined, starts at the level of the throat and forms folds down to the chest.

Forequarters: Strong bone structure, legs very muscular. Elbows neither turned in nor out too much. Forearm is straight or slightly inclined inward in order to get closer to the medium plane, especially with very broad chests. Pasterns are powerful, slightly

A handsome Dogue de Bordeaux, owned by Andrea Switzer. Photograph by Close Encounters of the Furry Kind, Bane and Jeannie Harrison.

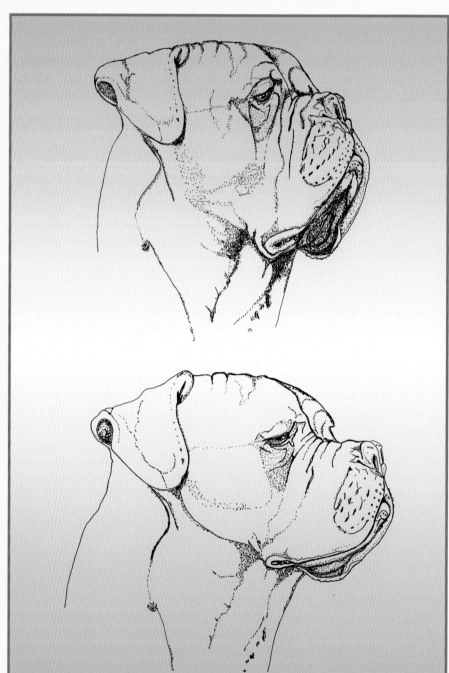

Correct head: square, pronounced indentation of stop, relatively short muzzle.

Incorrect head: longer rather than square, stop is not indented enough, muzzle is too long in relation to head.

sloping, sometimes a little turned. Feet are strong and tight. Nails curved and strong, preferably well pigmented. Pads well developed and supple.

Body: Chest is powerful, well ribbed up, broad, let down deeper than the elbows. Powerful fore-chest. Sternal ribs rounded. Other ribs well sprung and well let down. The circumference of the chest must be 0.25 m (about 9.8 in) to 0.30 m (11.8 in) superior to the height at the withers. Shoulders are powerful, muscles prominent, obliqueness of the shoulder blade about 45° to the horizontal. Angle of the scapular-humeral articulation a little more than 90°. Topline is straight, with a broad, muscular back. Withers well defined. Loin broad, rather short and solid. Rump moderately oblique down to the root of the tail. Underline is curved, from the long brisket to the tucked-up and firm abdomen.

Hindquarters: Thighs are well developed and thick, muscles visible. Stifle in a parallel plane to the vertical median plane or slightly turned inward or outward. Lower thigh is relatively short, muscular and well let down. Hock is short, sinewy, angle of the hock moderately open. When seen from behind, the parallel hind legs give the impres-sion of power, although the hindquarters are slightly less broad than the forequarters. Females: Identical characteristics, but less pronounced. Height is generally less than that of the males.

Tail: Very thick at the base. The tip does not reach below the hock. Carried low, deeply set. Hanging when at rest, generally raised from 90–121° in relation to this vertical position when dog is active.

Faults: Small head, not in propor-tion to the height at the withers, too long, narrow piped, round, oval, flat forehead. Absence of medial groove. Occipital protuber-ance too obvious. Naso-frontal angle too acute or too blunt. Wrinkles too close together, not mobile. Muzzle that is too long, too short, narrow, shallow, pointed, snipy (nose in front of lips). Muzzle parallel with the upper line of the skull, down-faced, fleshy below the eyes. Nose too narrow, tight nostrils, butterfly nose, dudley nose (flesh colored). Jaws of equal length (pinscher bite), scissors bite, overshot, exag-gerated or insufficient, undershot mouth. Teeth that are weak or badly lined up. Lips that are excessively long and floppy (non-retractable), too short. Under-developed cheeks, flabby, lean or gaunt. Eyes that are small, round, too sunken, protruding, close together, too light, staring expres-

The female Dogue, shown here, is slightly smaller than the male.

sion, showing haw. Ears too flabby, too short, too long, cropped, inset or carriage too high, pricked, rose ears, laterally set far apart, too low set. Slender, thin, long, or flat neck. Skin too tight or an exaggerated hanging dewlap. Narrow chest, not very long. Ribs too flat, or, on the contrary, barrel shaped. Brisket concave when seen from the front. Insufficiently muscled shoulders, or being too straight. Saddle back, humped back, weak loin, over-built rump, rump rounded or steeped. Tail that is carried sideways, truncated, broken twisted, docked, caudal vertebrate fused (knotted tail). Tail carried vertically or rolled up. Tufted tip.

Absence of tail, even accidental, is always suspect. Pendulous abdomen, or too tucked up. Forequarters of light bone, insufficient muscle. In or out too much at the elbows. Forearm too bowed. Pastern turned in or out too much, down in the pasterns. Flat, hare feet or splayed toes. Flat or thin hindquarters. Stifle too much turned out or in. Hock that is over angulated or too straight, dewclaws.

Facing page: Head study of a typical male Dogue.

Disqualifications: Wall eyed or flesh-colored spots on the eyelids.

Note: Male dogs should have two apparently normal testicles fully descended into the scrotum.

Dogue de Bordeaux

OWNER CONSIDERATIONS

How remarkable, unusual and alluring is the Dogue de Bordeaux! Who could deny the attention a pet owner would attract strolling through the neighborhood with a full-grown Dogue de Bordeaux? Not to mention the attention an irresistible Dogue puppy receives!

Who can resist a puppy...especially a breed as fascinating as the Dogue de Bordeaux?

Whether you are seeking a puppy simply as a home companion and family pet, a show dog, a hunting dog or a competition dog, there are many serious factors governing your choice. You believe that you have enough time to devote to your new Dogue de Bordeaux. Even a pet Dogue de Bordeaux will require considerable time to train. Naturally, a guard or obedience/agility dog will require hours of special training. Do not take the acquisition of a Dogue de Bordeaux lightly—everything about the Dogue is heavy! This is a demanding dog who will want to make you his number-one priority: Are you prepared for that commitment, which is accompanied by this giant's steadfast devotion, a bucket of drool, unabashed affection and a virtual ton of "poop"?

Consider the exercise that a dog as active as the Dogue de Bordeaux will require. You have a fenced yard, so there is no worry that your curious pup will not go wandering down the lane to find your neighbors and their dogs and cats and horses! If you are not committed to the welfare and whole existence of this powerful, purposeful animal; if, in the simplest, most basic example, you are not willing to walk your dog daily, despite the weather, do not choose a Dogue de Bordeaux as a companion.

Space is another huge consideration. The Dogue de Bordeaux in early puppyhood may be well accommodated in a corner of your kitchen but, after only six months, when the puppy is likely over 90 pounds, larger space certainly will be required. No matter how affectionate your Dogue puppy is in your company, he cannot exist in a two-room apartment. You will have to train your Dogue de Bordeaux to understand the house rules so that you can trust him in every room of your house. Of course, puppy-proofing for such a powerful animal is vital. The Dogue de Bordeaux can likely eat anything he wants—from his dog food to your slippers to your bedroom furniture!

There are the usual problems associated with puppies of any breed, like the damages likely to be sustained by your floors, furniture and flowers, and, not least of all, restrictions to your freedom (of movement), as in vacation or weekend trips. With the Dogue de Bordeaux, these demands and potential hazards are multiplied tenfold. This union is a serious affair and should be deeply considered but, once decided, your choice of a Dogue de Bordeaux can be the most reward-ing of all. A few suggestions will help in the purchase of your dog.

ACQUIRING A PUPPY

The recommended method of obtaining a pure-bred puppy of any breed is to seek out a reputable breeder. Given the relative rarity of the Dogue de Bordeaux, there are not as many breeders as there are with more

ARE YOU PREPARED?
Unfortunately, when a puppy is bought by someone who does not take into consideration the time and attention that dog ownership requires, it is the puppy who suffers when he is either abandoned or placed in a shelter by a frustrated owner. So all of the "homework" you do in preparation for your pup's arrival will benefit you both. The more informed you are, the more you will know what to expect and the better equipped you will be to handle the ups and downs of raising a puppy. Hopefully, everyone in the household is willing to do his part in raising and caring for the pup. The anticipation of owning a dog often brings a lot of promises from excited family members: "I will walk him every day," "I will feed him," "I will house-train him," etc., but these things take time and effort, and promises can easily be forgotten once the novelty of the new pet has worn off.

numerous breeds. Nonetheless, you will still have to conduct a thorough search to distinguish between reputable, ethical breeders and those that are irresponsible and profit-motivated. Such irresponsible breeders may advertise in the local newspapers. Generally these inexperienced people are probably kind enough toward their dogs, but do not have the expertise or facilities required to successfully raise a litter of Dogue puppies. Lack of attention to selective breeding can perpetuate genetic problems in the breed. A lack of proper feeding can cause indigestion, rickets, weak bones, poor teeth and other problems. Veterinary bills may soon distort initial savings into financial or, worse, emotional loss. More often than not, these breeders sell puppies at the same price as a conscientious breeder, so there is never a savings.

The Dogue de Bordeaux, a popular but rare breed, has yet to attract a large number of breeders, so the majority of breeders are both reliable and fair, with the breed's best interests first and foremost in their breeding programs. The best dogs of course are bred on the Continent, in France, the breed's homeland, as well as in Holland and Germany. Many breeders specialize in lines from these countries, so it is quite possible to acquire a well-bred Dogue de Bordeaux from these breeders.

When you visit the breeder, you will have ample opportunity to evaluate the puppies, the dam and the facility. Whenever possible, the breeder will present the dam, and hopefully the sire, to you. Viewing the parents of your chosen litter speaks volumes about the expected future quality, temperament, size, etc., of the pups. Actually meeting the dam is better than any promise the breeder could make regarding the excellence of the litter. Always keep in mind that the dam may appear somewhat bedraggled and "overworked." Caring for a large litter of Bordeaux pups for six to eight weeks could drain the life out of any bitch! Don't expect her to resemble the lovely photographs in this book. She has been working hard for months.

TEMPERAMENT COUNTS

Your selection of a good puppy can be determined by your needs. A show potential or a good pet? It is your choice. Every puppy, however, should be of good temperament. Although show-quality puppies are bred and raised with emphasis on physical conformation, responsible breeders strive for equally good temperament. Do not buy from a breeder who concentrates solely on physical beauty at the expense of personality.

When evaluating the litter, note the way the puppies move. The Dogue de Bordeaux, even in puppyhood, should show a fair amount of coordination. Despite the breed's giant stature, the Dogue is an athletic and agile animal. Don't expect the pup to be light on his big feet, but there should be no tendency to stumble or drag the hind feet. Look at the mouth to make sure that the bite is undershot, meaning that the lower jaw protrudes further than the upper jaw, as in that of a Bulldog, though not as exaggerated. If you have any doubts, ask to see the parents' mouths.

Consider the temperament of the litter. The pups should be friendly and outgoing, interested in their surroundings and amenable to handling. With a dog as large as the Dogue, temperament is of

Selecting from a litter of Dogues is not an easy task. Not only do you want the pup whose personality best suits you, but you want one who is healthy and sound.

paramount importance. While you want a Dogue de Bordeaux that is handsome, impressive and totally representative of the breed, you also want a Dogue that is friendly, trustworthy and 100% reliable around children. Given the power of this dog, you cannot afford to sacrifice the temperament of your chosen puppy. If the puppy has been properly socialized (that is, introduced to people, other dogs, situations outside his whelping pen), he should be personable and alert. Avoid a shy, overly aggressive or "spooky" puppy. If this

PUPPY APPEARANCE

Your puppy should have a well-fed appearance but not a distended abdomen, which may indicate worms or incorrect feeding, or both. The body should be firm, with a solid feel. The skin of the abdomen should be pale pink and clean, without signs of scratching or rash.

describes the whole litter, it's time to visit a new breeder. Bordeaux pups are absolutely delicious, irresistible and disarmingly adorable—don't be seduced by a litter that is not stable and friendly. That is your most important consideration.

PEDIGREE VS. REGISTRATION CERTIFICATE

Too often new owners are confused between these two important documents. Your puppy's pedigree, essentially a family tree, is a written record of a dog's genealogy of three generations or more. The pedigree will show you the names as well as performance titles of all the dogs in your pup's background. Your breeder must provide you with a registration application, with his part properly filled out. You must complete the application and send it to the registering organization (such as the UKC or ARBA) with the proper fee.

The seller must provide you with complete records to identify the puppy. The seller must provide the buyer with the following: breed; sex, color and markings; date of birth; litter number (when available); names and registration numbers of the parents; breeder's name; and date sold or delivered. The breeder must also document this information for his own records, as well as have proper health documentation for the pups.

COMMITMENT OF OWNERSHIP

After considering all of these factors, you have most likely already made some very important decisions about selecting your puppy. You have chosen the Dogue, which means that you have decided which characteristics you want in a dog and what type of dog will best fit into your family and lifestyle. If you have selected a breeder, you have gone a step further—you have done your research and found a responsible, conscientious person who breeds quality Dogues and who should be a reliable source of help as you and your puppy adjust to life together. If you have observed a litter in action, you have gotten a firsthand look at the dynamics of a puppy "pack" and, thus, you have learned about each pup's individual personality—perhaps you have even found one that particularly appeals to you.

However, even if you have not yet found the Dogue puppy of your dreams, observing pups will help you learn to recognize certain behavior and to determine what a pup's behavior indicates about his temperament. You will be able to pick out which pups are the leaders, which ones are less outgoing, which ones are confident, which ones are shy, playful, friendly, aggressive, etc. Equally important, you will learn to recognize how a healthy pup should look and act. All of these

Although these pups are little more than a handful now, Dogues de Bordeaux grow quickly and will become very large animals. They take up a lot of space, they have big appetites and they need exercise every day. Are you up to this responsibility?

things will help you in your search, and when you find the Dogue that was meant for you, you will know it!

Researching your breed, selecting a responsible breeder and observing as many pups as possible are all important steps on the way to dog ownership. It may seem like a lot of effort...and you have not even brought the pup home yet! Remember, though, you cannot be too careful when deciding on the type of dog you want and finding out about your prospective pup's background. Buying a puppy is not—or *should* not be—just another whimsical purchase. In fact, this is one instance in which you actually do get to choose your

TIME TO GO HOME
Breeders rarely release puppies until they are eight to ten weeks of age. This is an acceptable age for most breeds of dog, excepting toy breeds, which are not released until around 12 weeks, given their petite sizes. If a breeder has a puppy that is 12 weeks of age or older, it is likely well socialized and house-trained. Be sure that it is otherwise healthy before deciding to take it home.

You should have the opportunity to see the Dogue puppy with at least one of his parents, giving you a good idea of the pup's future size, looks and personality.

YOUR SCHEDULE . . .

If you lead an erratic, unpredictable life, with daily or weekly changes in your work requirements, consider the problems of owning a puppy. The new puppy has to be fed regularly, socialized (loved, petted, handled, introduced to other people) and, most importantly, allowed to go outdoors for house-training. As the dog gets older, he can be more tolerant of deviations in his feeding and relief schedule.

own family! But, you may be thinking, buying a puppy should be fun—it should not be so serious and so much work. If you keep in mind that your puppy is not a cuddly stuffed toy or decorative lawn ornament, but a real member of your family, you will realize that, while buying a puppy is a pleasurable and exciting endeavor, it is not something to be taken lightly. Relax...the fun will start when the pup comes home!

Always keep in mind that a puppy is nothing more than a baby in a furry disguise…a baby who is virtually helpless in a human world and who trusts his owner for fulfillment of his basic needs for survival. That goes beyond food, water and shelter; your pup needs care, protection, guidance and love. If you are not prepared to commit to this, then you are not prepared to own a dog of any breed.

"Wait a minute," you say. "How hard could this be? All of my neighbors own dogs and they seem to be doing just fine. Why should I have to worry about all of this?" Well, you should not worry about it; in fact, you will probably find that once your Dogue pup gets used to his new home, he will fall into his place in the family quite naturally. But it never hurts to emphasize the commitment of dog ownership. With some time and patience, it is really not too difficult to raise a curious and exuberant Dogue pup to be a well-adjusted and well-mannered adult dog—a dog that could be your most loyal friend.

It won't be long before this Dogue baby is too big to be carried around!

PREPARING PUPPY'S PLACE IN YOUR HOME

Researching your breed and finding a breeder are only two aspects of the "homework" you will have to do before bringing your Dogue puppy home. You will also have to prepare your home and family for the new addition. Much as you would prepare a nursery for a newborn baby, you will need to designate a place in your home that will be the puppy's own. How you prepare your home will depend on how much freedom the

ARE YOU A FIT OWNER?
If the breeder from whom you are buying a puppy asks you a lot of personal questions, do not be insulted. Such a breeder wants to be sure that you will be a fit provider for his puppy.

Puppies often stay in newspaper-lined areas before they are old enough to relieve themselves outside their living quarters. You'll want to avoid lining your pup's crate at home with newspaper or he may get into the habit of soiling his crate.

has ever known, so it is important to make his transition as easy as possible. By preparing a place in your home for the puppy, you are making him feel as welcome as possible in a strange new place. It should not take him long to get used to it, but the sudden shock of being transplanted is somewhat traumatic for a young pup. Imagine how a small child would feel in the same situation—that is how your puppy must be feeling. It is up to you to reassure him and to let him know, "Little fellow, you are going to like it here!"

WHAT YOU SHOULD BUY
CRATE

To someone unfamiliar with the use of crates in dog training, it may seem like punishment to shut a dog in a crate. This is not the case at all. Although all breeders do not advocate crate training, more and more breeders and trainers are recommending crates as preferred tools for pet puppies as well as show puppies. Crates are not cruel—crates have many

dog will be allowed. Will he be granted full run of the house or have access to certain rooms only? Whatever you decide, you must ensure that he has a place that he can "call his own."

When you bring your new puppy into your home, you are bringing him into what will become his home as well. Obviously, you did not buy a puppy so that he could take control of the house, but in order for a puppy to grow into a stable, well-adjusted dog, he has to feel comfortable in his surroundings. Remember, he is leaving the warmth and security of his mother and littermates, plus the familiarity of the only place he

QUALITY FOOD
The cost of food must be mentioned. All dogs need a good-quality food with an adequate supply of protein to develop their bones and muscles properly. Most dogs are not picky eaters but, unless fed properly, can quickly succumb to skin problems.

humane and highly effective uses in dog care and training. For example, crate training is a much-recommended and successful housebreaking method, a crate can keep your dog safe during travel and, perhaps most importantly, a crate provides your dog with a place of his own in your home. It serves as a "doggie bedroom" of sorts—your Dogue can curl up in his crate when he wants to sleep or when he just needs a rest. Many dogs sleep in their crates overnight. When lined with soft blankets and with his favorite toy or a stuffed pal, a crate becomes a cozy pseudo-den for your dog. Like his ancestors, he too will seek out the comfort and retreat of a den—you just happen to be providing him with something a little more luxurious than leaves and twigs lining a dirty ditch.

As far as purchasing a crate, the type that you buy is up to you. It will most likely be one of the two most popular types: wire or fiberglass. The wire crate is more open,

allowing the air to flow through and affording the dog a view of what is going on around him. A fiberglass crate is sturdier and is preferable as a travel crate since it provides more protection for the

Most pet shops have a large variety of crates in all sizes, styles and types. You need the largest size for your Dogue puppy, because he will grow into such a large dog.

Wicker dog beds are satisfactory for very young puppies, but when they start to chew, the wicker will be the first to go!

CRATE-TRAINING TIPS

During crate training, you should partition off the section of the crate in which the pup stays. If he is given too big an area, this will hinder your training efforts. Crate training is based on the fact that a dog does not like to soil his sleeping quarters, so it is ineffective to keep a pup in an area that is so big that he can eliminate in one end and get far enough away from it to sleep. Also, you want to make the crate den-like for the pup. Blankets and a favorite toy will make the crate cozy for the small pup; as he grows, you may want to evict some of his "roommates" to make more room. It will take some coaxing at first, but be patient. Given some time to get used to it, your pup will adapt to his new home-within-a-home quite nicely.

The puppy's bedding is important. Take the advice of the breeder as to what you should use to make your puppy comfortable.

dog. The size of the crate is another thing to consider. Puppies do not stay puppies forever—in fact, sometimes it seems as if they grow right before your eyes. A medium-sized crate may be fine for a very young Dogue pup, but it will not do him much good for long! Unless you have the money and the inclination to buy a new crate every time your pup has a growth spurt, it is better to get one that will accommodate your dog both as a pup and at full size. The largest crate available will be

necessary for a full-grown Dogue de Bordeaux.

BEDDING

A soft lambswool pad in the dog's crate will help the dog feel more at home and you may also like to give him a blanket. This will take the place of the leaves, twigs, etc., that the pup would use in the wild to make a den, and the pup can make his own "burrow" in the crate. Although your pup is far removed from his den-making ancestors, the denning instinct is still a part of his genetic makeup. Until you bring your pup home, he has been sleeping amid the warmth of his mother and litter-mates, and while a blanket is not the same as a warm, breathing body, it still provides heat and something with which to snuggle. You will want to wash your pup's

TOYS, TOYS, TOYS!

With a big variety of dog toys available, and so many that look like they would be a lot of fun for a dog, be careful in your selection. It is amazing what a set of puppy teeth can do to an innocent-looking toy; so, obviously, safety is a major consideration. Be sure to choose the most durable products that you can find. Hard nylon bones and toys are a safe bet, and many of them are offered in different scents and flavors that will be sure to capture your dog's attention. It is always fun to play a game of fetch with your dog, and there are balls and flying discs that are specially made to withstand dog teeth.

Toys that may suit a young Dogue puppy can be easily destroyed as the pup grows bigger. Purchase sturdy toys appropriate to your Dogue's size and strength.

bedding frequently in case he has a potty accident in his crate, and replace or remove any blanket or padding that becomes ragged and starts to fall apart.

One of the best chew devices is heavy nylon rope that has been boiled to anneal the threads and flavored to make it attractive to dogs. It not only is entertaining but it also reduces plaque on the Dogue's teeth.

TOYS

Toys are a must for dogs of all ages, especially for curious playful pups. Puppies are the "children" of the dog world, and what child does not love toys? Chew toys provide enjoyment to both dog and owner—your dog will enjoy playing with his favorite toys, while you will enjoy the fact that they distract him from your expensive shoes and leather sofa. Puppies love to chew. In fact, chewing is a physical need for pups when they are teething, and everything looks appetizing! The full range of your possessions— from old dishcloth to Oriental

Pet shops carry many special toys made for dogs. Do not offer toys made for humans to your pet.

rug—are fair game in the eyes of a teething pup. Puppies are not discerning when it comes to finding something to literally "sink their teeth into"—everything tastes great!

Dogues of all ages like to chew, and they have very powerful jaws and teeth. Purchase only the most durable chews, such as hard nylon bones, for your Dogue, and make sure all toys are of the appropriate size. A large dog like the Dogue can easily swallow small bones and balls, so purchase toys designed for large breeds.

Stuffed toys can be put in the dog's crate to give him some company, but be careful of these, as a pup can de-stuff one pretty quickly. Stay away from stuffed toys with small plastic eyes or other parts that could choke a pup. Similarly, squeaky toys are

You should be prepared with a suitable crate, toys, water and food bowls and a few other essentials *before* you bring home the Dogue puppy.

quite popular. There are dogs that will come running from anywhere in the house at the first sound from their favorite squeaky friend, but if a pup de-stuffs one of these, the small plastic squeaker inside can be dangerous if swallowed. Adult Dogues will have no trouble destroying a soft or squeaky toy in short order. Monitor the condition of your dog's toys carefully and get rid of any that have been chewed to the point of becoming potentially dangerous.

Be careful of natural bones, which have a tendency to splinter into sharp, dangerous pieces. Also be careful of rawhide, which can turn into pieces that are easy to swallow or a mushy mess on your carpet.

While thin leads like this are suitable for very young Dogue puppies, they are not strong enough for regular walks and exercise.

Your pet shop should have a complete stock of leads from which you can select the one most suitable for the size of your Dogue.

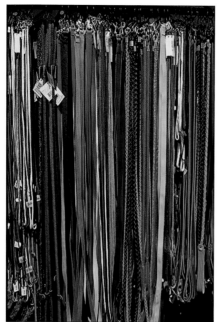

As your Dogue grows, his collar should not just be larger, but made of stronger material as well.

LEAD

A nylon lead is probably the best option, as it is the most resistant to puppy teeth should your pup take a liking to chewing on his lead. This habit should be nipped in the bud, but if your pup likes to chew on his lead, he has a very slim chance of being able to chew through strong nylon. Nylon leads are also lightweight, which is good for a young Dogue who is just getting used to the idea of walking on a lead. For everyday walking and safety purposes, the nylon lead is a good choice.

There are special leads for training purposes, and specially made harnesses for the working Dogue, but these are not necessary

When buying a collar for your Dogue puppy, keep in mind that the puppy will grow quickly and the collar must increase in size to keep pace with this growth.

for routine walks. As your Dogue matures, you will need to purchase something stronger, like a thicker leather lead.

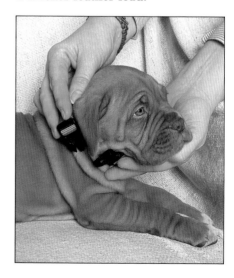

The **BUCKLE COLLAR** is the standard collar used for everyday purposes. Be sure that you adjust the buckle on growing puppies. Check it every day. It can become too tight overnight! These collars can be made of leather or nylon. Attach your dog's identification tags to this collar.

BUCKLE COLLAR

CHOKE COLLAR

The **CHOKE COLLAR** is designed for training. It is constructed of highly polished steel so that it slides easily through the stainless steel loop. The idea is that the dog controls the pressure around his neck and he will stop pulling if the collar becomes uncomfortable. *Never* leave a choke collar on your dog when not training.

The **HALTER** is for a trained dog that has to be restrained to prevent running away, chasing a cat and the like. Considered the most humane of all collars, it is frequently used on smaller dogs for which collars are not comfortable.

HALTER

Your local pet shop should carry a variety of dog bowls. Sturdy plastic bowls are very popular, as well as more chew-resistant stainless steel and heavy crockery bowls.

COLLAR

Your pup should get used to wearing a collar at all times since you will want to attach his ID tags to his collar and you have to attach the lead to something! Make sure that the collar fits snugly enough so that the pup cannot wriggle out of it, but is loose enough so that it will not be uncomfortably tight around the pup's neck. You should be able to fit a finger between the pup and the collar. It may take some time for your pup to get used to wearing the collar, but soon he will not even notice that it is there. The choke collar is made for training, but should only be used by those who know exactly how to use it. If you use a stronger leather lead or a chain lead to walk your Dogue, you will also need a stronger collar.

FOOD AND WATER BOWLS

Your pup will need two bowls, one for food and one for water. You may want two sets of bowls, one for inside and one for outside, depending on where the dog will be fed and where he will be spending most of his time. Stainless steel or sturdy plastic bowls are popular choices. Plastic bowls are more chewable, and dogs tend not to chew on the steel variety, which can be sanitized. Dogue owners should put their dogs' food and water bowls on specially made elevated stands. This brings the food closer to the dog's level so he does not have to bend down as far, aiding his digestion and helping to guard against bloat (gastric torsion). It is important to buy sturdy bowls since everything is in danger of being chewed by puppy teeth and you do not want your dog to be constantly chewing apart his bowl (for his safety and for your wallet!).

CLEANING SUPPLIES
Plan on doing a lot of cleaning until your pup is house-trained. "Accidents" will occur, which is okay for now because the pup does not know any better. All you can do is be prepared to clean up any accidents—old rags, towels, newspapers and a safe disinfectant are good to have on hand.

Tools like this will take the work out of cleaning up after your dog. Make it a habit to clean up whenever your dog relieves himself, regardless of where it occurs.

BEYOND THE BASICS
The items previously discussed are the bare necessities. You will discover what else you need as you go along—grooming supplies, flea/tick protection, baby gates to partition a room, etc.—these things will vary depending on your situation. In the beginning, though, it is important that you have everything you need to feed and make your Dogue comfortable in his first few days at home.

PUPPY-PROOFING YOUR HOME
Aside from making sure that your Dogue will be comfortable in your home, you also have to make sure that your home is safe for your Dogue. This means taking precautions to make sure that your pup will not get into anything he

---

FINANCIAL RESPONSIBILITY
Grooming tools, collars, leashes, a crate, a dog bed and, of course, toys will be expenses to you when you first obtain your pup, and the cost will continue throughout your dog's lifetime. If your puppy damages or destroys your possessions (as most puppies surely will!) or something belonging to a neighbor, you can calculate additional expense. There is also flea and pest control, which every dog owner faces more than once. You must be able to handle the financial responsibility of owning a dog.

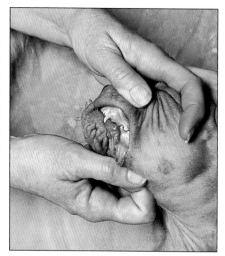

Examine your Dogue's teeth regularly. All dogs must chew to help their teeth grow in straight and strong and to keep them clean. Chewing also exercises the jaw muscles.

should not get into and that there is nothing within his reach that may harm him should he sniff it, chew it, inspect it, etc. While you are primarily concerned with your pup's safety, you do not want your belongings to be ruined. Breakables should be placed out of reach if your dog is to have full run of the house. If he is to be limited to certain

SKULL & CROSSBONES

Thoroughly puppy-proof your house before bringing your puppy home. Never use cockroach or rodent poisons or plant fertilizers in any area accessible to the puppy. Avoid the use of toilet cleaners. Most dogs are born with "toilet-bowl sonar" and will take a drink if the lid is left open. Also keep the trash secured and out of reach.

places within the house, keep any potentially dangerous items in the "off-limits" areas. Electrical cords should be fastened tightly against the wall, out of puppy's reach. They can pose a danger should the puppy decide to taste them—and who is going to convince a pup that loose wires would not make great chew toys? If your dog is going to spend time in a crate, make sure that there is nothing near his crate that he can reach if he sticks his curious little nose or paws through the openings. Just as you would with a child, keep all household cleaners and chemicals where the pup cannot get to them.

It is just as important to make sure that the outside of your home is safe. Your puppy should never be unsupervised, but a pup let loose in the yard will want to run and explore, and he should be granted that freedom. Do not let a fence give you a false sense of security; you would be surprised how crafty (and persistent) a dog can be in figuring out how to dig under or climb over a fence. The remedy is to make the fence high enough so that it really is impossible for your dog to get over it (about 6–7 feet should suffice), and well embedded into the ground. Be sure to repair or secure any gaps in the fence and check the fence periodically to ensure that it remains in good shape. A very determined pup may return to the same spot to "work on it" until he is able to get through.

FIRST TRIP TO THE VET

You have picked out your puppy, your home and family are ready, now all you have to do is pick your Dogue up from the breeder

and the fun begins, right? Well…not so fast. You also need to prepare for your pup's first trip to the veterinarian. Perhaps the breeder can recommend someone in the area who specializes in large breeds, or maybe you know some other Dogue owners who can suggest a good vet. Either way, you should have an appointment arranged for your pup before you pick him up, and plan on taking him for a check-up before bringing him home.

The pup's first visit will consist of an overall examination to make sure that the pup does not have any problems that are not apparent to you. The veterinarian will also set up a schedule for the pup's vaccinations. The breeder will inform you of which ones the pup has already received and the vet can continue from there.

INTRODUCTION TO THE FAMILY

Everyone in the house will be excited about the puppy's coming home and will want to pet him and play with him, but it is best to make the introductions low-key so as not to overwhelm the puppy. He is already apprehensive. It is the first time he has been separated from his mother and the breeder, and the ride to your home is likely the first time he has been in a car. The last thing you want to do is smother him, as

Plan a trip to the vet as one of the first things you do with your new Dogue de Bordeaux puppy.

this will only frighten him further. Human contact is extremely necessary at this stage, because this is the time when a connection between the pup and his human family are formed. Gentle petting and soothing words should help console him, as will putting him down and letting him explore on his own (under your watchful eye, of course).

The pup may approach the family members or may busy himself with exploring for awhile. Gradually, each person should spend some time with the pup, one at a time, crouching down to get as close to the pup's level as possible while letting him sniff their hands and petting him gently. He needs human attention and he needs to be touched in order to form an immediate bond. Just remember that the pup is

experiencing a lot of things for the first time, at the same time. There are new people, new noises, new smells and new things to investigate, so be gentle, be affectionate and be as comforting as you can.

PUP'S FIRST NIGHT HOME

You have traveled home with your new charge safely in his basket or crate. He's been to the vet for a thorough check-up. He's been weighed, his papers examined; perhaps he's even been vaccinated and wormed. He's met the family, including the excited children and the less-than-happy cat. He's explored his area, his new bed, the yard and anywhere else he's been permitted. He's eaten his first meal at home and relieved himself in the proper place. He's heard lots of new sounds, smelled new friends and seen more of the outside world than ever before.

That was the just the first day! He's worn out and is ready for bed...or so you think!

It's puppy's first night and you are ready to say "Good night." Keep in mind that this is puppy's first night sleeping alone. His dam and littermates are no longer at paw's length and he's a bit scared, cold and lonely. Be reassuring to your new family member, but this is not the time to spoil him and give in to his inevitable whining.

Puppies whine. They whine to let others know where they are

THE RIDE HOME

Taking your dog from the breeder to your home in a car can be a very uncomfortable experience for both of you. The puppy will have been taken from his warm, friendly, safe environment—an environment that moves! Be prepared for loose bowels, urination, crying, whining and even fear biting. With proper love and encouragement when you arrive home, the stress of the trip should quickly disappear.

and to get company. Place your pup in his new bed or crate in his room and close the crate door. Mercifully, he may fall asleep without a peep. When the inevitable occurs, ignore the whining; he is fine. Be strong and keep his interest in mind. Do not become guilty and visit the pup. He will fall asleep eventually.

Many breeders recommend placing a piece of bedding from the pup's former home in his new bed so that he recognizes the scent of his littermates. Others still advise placing a hot-water bottle in his bed for warmth. The latter may be a good idea, provided the pup doesn't attempt to suckle—he'll get good and wet and may not fall asleep so fast. Puppy's first night can be some-what stressful for the pup and his new family. Remember that you are setting the tone of nighttime at your house. Unless you want to play with your pup every night at 10 pm, midnight and 2 am, don't initiate the habit. Your family will thank you, and soon so will your pup!

PREVENTING PUPPY PROBLEMS

Socialization

Now that you have done all of the preparatory work and have helped your pup get accustomed to his new home and family, it is time for you to have some fun! Socializing your Dogue pup gives

Your house is a big, unfamiliar place for a small Dogue puppy—especially on his first night. It will take him some time to get used to his new home.

you the opportunity to show off your new friend. Your pup gets to reap the benefits of being an adorable, intriguing creature that

THE COCOA WARS

Chocolate contains the chemical thebromine, which is poisonous to dogs, although "chocolates" especially made for dogs are safe (as they don't actually contain thebromine) but not recommended. Any item that encourages your dog to enjoy the taste of cocoa should be discouraged. You should also exercise caution when using mulch in your garden. This frequently contains cocoa hulls, and dogs have been known to die from eating mulch.

Whether a dog bed or a crate, make the place where your puppy sleeps comfortable.

people will want to pet and, in general, think is absolutely precious!

Besides getting to know his new family, your puppy should be exposed to other people, animals and situations, but of course he must not come into close contact with dogs you don't know well until his course of injections is fully complete. This will help him become well adjusted and less prone to being timid or fearful of the new things he will encounter. Your pup's socialization began at

---

NATURAL TOXINS

Examine your lawn and home landscaping before bringing your puppy home. Many varieties of plants have leaves, stems or flowers that are toxic if ingested, and you can depend on a curious puppy to investigate them. Ask your vet for information on poisonous plants or research them at your library.

---

the breeder's, but now it is your responsibility. The socialization he receives up until the age of 12 weeks is the most critical, as this is the time when he forms his impressions of the outside world. Be especially careful during the eight-to-ten-week-old period, known as the fear period. The interaction he receives during this time should be gentle and reassuring Lack of socialization can manifest itself in fear and aggression as the dog grows up. He needs lots of human interaction, affection, handling and exposure to other animals.

Once your pup has received his necessary vaccinations, feel free to take him out and about (on his lead, of course). Take him around the neighborhood, take him on your daily errands, let people pet him, let him meet other dogs and pets, etc. Puppies do not have to try to make friends. There will be no shortage of people who will want to introduce themselves. Just make sure that you carefully supervise each interaction. You want your dog to be comfortable around everyone.

If the neighborhood children want to say hello, for example, that is great. Children and pups most often make great companions, but sometimes an excited child can unintentionally handle a pup too roughly, or an overzealous pup can playfully nip a little too hard. You want to make socialization experiences positive ones. What a pup learns during this very formative stage will impact his attitude toward future encounters. A pup that has a bad experience with a child may grow up to be a dog that is shy around or aggressive toward children.

CONSISTENCY IN TRAINING

Dogs, being pack animals, need a leader or they will try to establish dominance in their packs. When you bring a dog into your family, who becomes the leader and who becomes the pack are entirely up to you! Your pup's intuitive quest for dominance, coupled with the fact that it is nearly impossible to look at an adorable Dogue pup with his "puppy-dog" eyes and not cave in, give the pup an unfair advantage in getting the upper hand! A pup will definitely test the waters to see what he can and cannot get away with. Do not give in to those pleading eyes—stand your ground when it comes to disciplining the pup and make sure that all family members do the same. Avoid discrepancies by having all members of the house-hold decide on the rules before the pup even comes home…and be consistent in enforcing them! It will only confuse the pup if Mom tells him to get off the couch when he is used to sitting up there with Dad to watch the nightly news. Early training shapes the dog's personality, so

Underneath that serious expression is a friendly, curious puppy who is eager to meet the world!

you cannot be unclear in what you expect.

COMMON PUPPY PROBLEMS

The best way to prevent problems is to be proactive in stopping an undesirable behavior as soon as it starts. The old saying "You can't teach an old dog new tricks" does

PUP MEETS WORLD

Thorough socialization includes not only meeting new people but also being introduced to new experiences such as riding in the car, having his coat brushed, hearing the television, walking in a crowd—the list is endless. The more your pup experiences, and the more positive the experiences are, the less of a shock and the less frightening it will be for your pup to encounter new things.

Face your developing puppy's education head-on. It's best to be prepared for a problem and its solution before it actually occurs.

not necessarily hold true, but it *is* true that it is much easier to discourage bad behavior in a young developing pup than to wait until the pup's bad behavior becomes the adult dog's bad habit. There are some problems that are especially prevalent in puppies as they develop.

NIPPING

As puppies start to teethe, they feel the need to sink their teeth into anything…including your fingers, arms, hair, and toes. You may find this behavior cute for the first five seconds, until you feel just how sharp those puppy teeth are. This is something you want to discourage immediately and consistently with a firm "No!" (or whatever number of firm "Nos" it takes for him to understand that you mean business). Then replace your finger with an appropriate chew toy. While this behavior is merely annoying when the dog is young, it can become dangerous as your Dogue's adult teeth grow in and his jaws develop if he is not taught that nipping is inappropriate. You do not want to take a chance with a Dogue, as this is a breed whose jaws become very strong. He does not mean any harm with a friendly nip, but he does not know his own strength.

CRYING/WHINING

Your pup will often cry, whine, whimper, howl or make some type of commotion when he is left alone. This is his way of calling out for attention to make sure that you know he is there and that you have not forgotten about him. He feels insecure when he is left alone, such as when you are out of the house and he is in

CHEWING TIPS

Chewing goes hand in hand with nipping in the sense that a teething puppy is always looking for a way to soothe his aching gums. In this case, instead of chewing on you, he may have taken a liking to your favorite shoe or something else that he should not be chewing. Again, realize that this is a normal canine behavior that does not need to be discouraged, only redirected. Your pup just needs to be taught what is acceptable to chew on and what is off-limits. Consistently tell him "No!" when you catch him chewing on something forbidden and give him a chew toy.

Conversely, praise him when you catch him chewing on something appropriate. In this way, you are discouraging the inappropriate behavior and reinforcing the desired behavior. The puppy's chewing should stop after his adult teeth have come in, but an adult dog continues to chew for various reasons—perhaps because he is bored, needs to relieve tension or just likes to chew. That is why it is important to redirect his chewing when he is still young.

Facing page: This Dogue de Bordeaux is the king of his castle! A dog house is a good way to provide shade and a place to rest for a dog that spends a lot of time outdoors.

his crate or when you are in another part of the house and he cannot see you. The noise he is making is an expression of the anxiety he feels at being alone, so he needs to be taught that being alone is okay. You are not actually training the dog to stop making noise, you are training him to feel comfortable when he is alone and removing the need for him to make noise.

When you are not there to supervise, the puppy is safer in his crate, with a cozy blanket and a toy, than roaming freely about the house. In order for the pup to stay in his crate without making a fuss, he needs to be comfortable there. It is extremely important that the crate is never used as a form of punishment, or the pup will develop a negative association with the crate.

Accustom the pup to the crate in short, gradually increasing time intervals in which you put him in the crate, maybe with a treat, and stay in the room with him. If he cries or makes a fuss, do not go to him, but stay in his sight. Gradually he will realize that staying in his crate is okay, and it will not be so traumatic for him when you are not around. You may want to leave the radio on softly when you leave the house; the sound of human voices may be comforting to him.

It is not recommended to baby your Dogue puppy when he cries and whines. He will never be trained to spend time alone if you come running every time he whimpers.

Your Dogue puppy will have been started on puppy food by the breeder. You should continue to feed your puppy this diet, and your vet will advise you of recommended dietary changes at the appropriate times.

DIETARY AND FEEDING CONSIDERATIONS

You have probably heard it a thousand times: "You are what you eat." Believe it or not, it's very true. Dogs are what you feed them because they have little choice in the matter. Even those people who truly want to feed

their dogs the best often can't do so because they do not know which foods are best for their dogs.

Dog foods are produced in three basic types: dry, semi-moist and canned. Dry foods are useful for the cost-conscious because they are more economical than semi-moist and canned. Dry foods contain the least fat and the most preservatives. Most canned foods are 60–70% water, while semi-moist foods are so full of sugar that they are the least preferred by owners, though dogs welcome them (as a child does candy).

Three stages of development must be considered when selecting a diet for your dog: the puppy stage, the adult stage and the senior stage.

Puppy Stage

Puppies have a natural instinct to suckle milk from their mother's nipples. They should exhibit this behavior the first day of their lives. If they don't suckle within a few hours, the breeder will attempt to put them onto the nipples. If they fail to suckle, the breeder must hand-feed them under the advice and guidance of

Puppies have a strong natural instinct for suckling. Their mother's milk is optimal nutrition for the first weeks of their lives.

a veterinarian. This will involve a baby bottle and a special formula. Although there are some excellent formulas available, mother's milk is best because it contains colostrum, an antibiotic milk that protects the puppies during the first eight to ten weeks of their lives.

Puppies should be allowed to nurse for about the first six weeks, although, starting around the third or fourth week, the breeder will begin to introduce small portions of suitable solid food. Most breeders like to introduce alternate milk and meat meals initially, building up to weaning time.

By the time they are seven or a maximum of eight weeks old,

TEST FOR PROPER DIET
A good test for proper diet is the color, odor and firmness of your dog's stool. A healthy dog usually produces three semi-hard stools per day. The stools should have no unpleasant odor. They should be the same color from excretion to excretion.

they should be completely weaned and fed solely a quality puppy food. During this time, selection of the pup's diet is most important as the puppy grows fastest during his first year of life. A Dogue de Bordeaux puppy will have a hearty appetite as soon as he becomes accustomed to his new home, and it is essential that he receives the best nutrition possible. If proper nutrition is not provided in the crucial growth stage of puppyhood, it may cause deficiencies that cannot be compensated for later in life. Never mistake overfeeding for proper nutrition.

Young Dogue de Bordeaux puppies should not be allowed to eat beyond their own portions, paying special attention to avoiding table food. Excessive weight on a Bordeaux pup can do irreparable harm to his growing joints. It's far better to have your Bordeaux slightly underweight than to fatten him up.

FEEDING TIPS

Dog food must be served at room temperature, neither too hot nor too cold. Fresh water, changed often and served in a clean bowl, is mandatory, although you should limit your Dogue's water intake at mealtimes and *never* allow him to gulp water at any time.

Never feed your dog from the table while you are eating, and never feed your dog leftovers from your own meal. They usually contain too much fat and too much seasoning.

Dogs must chew their food. Hard pellets are excellent; soups and stews are to be avoided. Don't add any extras to normal dog food, as it is usually balanced, and adding something extra destroys the balance.

Except for age-related changes, dogs do not require dietary variations. They can be fed the same diet, day after day, without becoming bored or ill.

Some dog owners like to cook for their dogs; however, it's easier to provide proper nutrition with a complete dog food than to try to figure out the right balance on your own.

Puppy diets should be balanced for your dog's needs, and supplements of vitamins, minerals and protein should not be necessary, and, in fact, can be harmful. Discuss supplements with your vet and breeder before offering any to your Dogue.

ADULT DIETS

A dog is considered an adult when he has stopped growing in height and/or length. Do not consider the dog's weight when making the decision to switch from a puppy diet to a maintenance diet. You should rely upon your vet or breeder to recommend an acceptable maintenance diet and to advise you on when to make the switch. A Dogue de Bordeaux reaches full physical maturity at about two years of age, though some dogs may take up to three years. The switch to adult food will be made before this time; the exact age can vary according to the dog's individual growth and development.

Major dog-food manufacturers specialize in adult-maintenance foods and it is necessary for you to select the one best suited to your dog's needs. Active dogs may have different requirements than more sedate dogs.

SENIOR DIETS

As dogs get older, their metabolism changes. The older dog usually exercises less, moves

> **GRAIN-BASED DIETS**
> Some less expensive dog foods are based on grains and other plant proteins. While these products may appear to be attractively priced, many breeders prefer a diet based on animal proteins and believe that they are more conducive to your dog's health. Many grain-based diets rely on soy protein, which may cause flatulence (passing gas).
>
> There are many cases, however, when your dog might require a special diet. These special requirements should only be recommended by your veterinarian.

more slowly and sleeps more. This change in lifestyle and physiological performance requires a change in diet. Since these changes take place slowly, they

Nursing bitches may require supplements to their diets. Don't go about this yourself—always consult your vet for nutritional advice.

A WORTHY INVESTMENT

Veterinary studies have proved that a high-quality diet pays off in your dog's coat quality, behavior and activity level. Invest in premium brands for the maximum payoff with your dog.

might not be recognizable. What is easily recognizable is weight gain. Continuing to feed your dog an adult-maintenance diet when he is slowing down metabolically will cause him to gain weight. Obesity in an older dog compounds the health problems that already accompany old age.

As your dog gets older, few of his organs function up to par. The kidneys slow down and the intestines become less efficient. These age-related factors are best handled with a change in diet and a change in feeding schedule to give smaller portions that are more easily digested.

There is no single best diet for every older dog. While many dogs do well on light or senior diets, other dogs do better on puppy diets or special premium diets such as lamb and rice. Be sensitive to your senior Dogue de Bordeaux's diet, and this will help control other problems that may arise with your old friend.

WATER

Just as your dog needs proper nutrition from his food, water is an essential "nutrient" as well. Water keeps the dog's body properly hydrated and promotes normal function of the body's systems. During housebreaking, it is necessary to keep an eye on how much water your Dogue de Bordeaux is drinking but, once he is reliably trained, he should have

access to clean fresh water at all times. Make sure that the dog's water bowl is clean and elevated on a bowl stand, and change the water often, making sure that water is always available for your dog (although restricted at meal-times, as a bloat preventative).

"Have you got something there for me?" Some dogs are always looking for a treat!

EXERCISE

All dogs require some form of exercise, regardless of breed. A sedentary lifestyle is as harmful to a dog as it is to a person. The Dogue de Bordeaux happens to be an active breed that requires and enjoys exercise, but you don't have to be an Olympic athlete to provide your dog with the exercise he needs. Regular walks, play sessions in the fenced yard, or letting the dog run free in a secure enclosure under your supervision are all sufficient forms of exercise for the Dogue de Bordeaux. For those who are more ambitious, you will find that your adult Dogue will be able to keep up

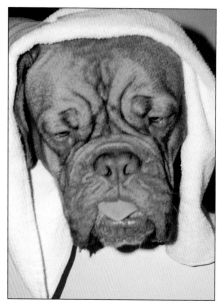

Bathing a Dogue de Bordeaux requires plenty of patience, time and towels! Don't forget to clean the facial wrinkles too.

with you on extra-long walks or a morning run. Always keep in mind that exercise should be restricted for at least an hour before and after mealtime.

Remember that exercise is not only essential to keep the dog's body fit, it is essential to his mental well-being. A bored dog will find something to do, which often manifests itself in some type of destructive behavior. In this sense, it is just as essential for the owner's mental well-being!

GROOMING

BRUSHING

The Dogue de Bordeaux's coat is short and close, and does not require much grooming to maintain. Regular once-overs with a brush or grooming glove will keep the coat looking shiny and healthy. Brushing is effective for removing any dead hair, dandruff or debris from the coat, and it stimulates the dog's skin and natural oils. Regular grooming sessions are also a good way to spend time with your dog. Many dogs grow to like the feel of being brushed and enjoy the daily routine.

BATHING

Dogs do not need to be bathed as often as humans, but bathing as needed is essential for healthy skin and a clean, shiny coat. If you accustom your pup to being bathed as a puppy, it will be second nature by the time he grows up. You want your dog to be at ease in the bath or it could end up a wet, soapy, messy ordeal for both of you!

Brush your Dogue de Bordeaux thoroughly before

SOAP IT UP

The use of human soap products like shampoo, bubble bath and hand soap can be damaging to a dog's coat and skin. Human products are too strong; they remove the protective oils coating the dog's hair and skin that make him water-resistant. Use only shampoo made especially for dogs. You may like to use a medicated shampoo, which will help to keep external parasites at bay.

Healthy dog hairs enlarged about 200 times their natural size. The inset shows a growing tip. Scanning electron micrographs by Dr. Dennis Kunkel, University of Hawaii.

Your local pet shop will have a selection of grooming tools. Your Dogue will not require excessive grooming, but you'll want to have the basics handy for maintaining his short coat.

Once accustomed to it, your Dogue puppy will enjoy the feel of being groomed with a soft brush or glove.

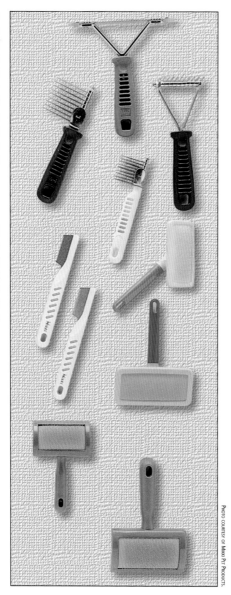

PHOTO COURTESY OF MIKKI PET PRODUCTS.

or hose attachment is necessary for thoroughly wetting and rinsing the coat. Check the water temperature to make sure that it is neither too hot nor too cold.

Next, apply shampoo to the dog's coat and work it into a good lather. You should purchase a shampoo that is made for dogs; do not use a product made for human hair. Wash the head last. You do not want shampoo to drip

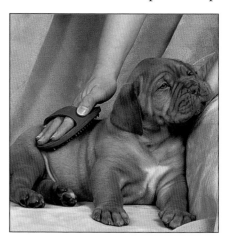

into the dog's eyes while you are washing the rest of his body. Work the shampoo all the way down to the skin. You can use this opportunity to check the skin for any bumps, bites or other abnormalities. Do not neglect any area of the body—get all of the hard-to-reach places.

Once the dog has been thoroughly shampooed, he requires an equally thorough rinsing. Shampoo left in the coat can be

wetting his coat. Make sure that your dog has a good non-slip surface to stand on. Begin by wetting the dog's coat. A shower

irritating to the skin. Protect his eyes from the shampoo by shielding them with your hand and directing the flow of water in the opposite direction. You should also avoid getting water in the ear canal. Be prepared for your dog to shake out his coat—you might want to stand back, but make sure you have a hold on the dog to keep him from running through the house, and have a towel ready.

EAR CLEANING

The ears should be kept clean and any excess hair inside the ear should be trimmed. Ears can be cleaned with a cotton ball and an ear-cleaning product made especially for dogs. Be on the lookout for any signs of infection or ear-mite infestation. If your Dogue de Bordeaux has been shaking his head or scratching at his ears frequently, this usually indicates a problem. If his ears have an unusual odor, this is a sure sign of mite infestation or infection, and a signal to have his ears checked by the veterinarian.

NAIL CLIPPING

Your Dogue de Bordeaux should be accustomed to having his nails trimmed at an early age, since it will be a part of your maintenance routine throughout his life. Not only does it look nicer, but a dog with long nails can cause injury if he jumps up or scratches some-

BATHING BEAUTY

Once you are sure that the dog is thoroughly rinsed, squeeze the excess water out of his coat with your hand and dry him with a heavy towel. You may choose to use a blow dryer set on "low" on his coat or just let it dry naturally. In cold weather, never allow your dog outside with a wet coat.

There are "dry bath" products on the market, which are sprays and powders intended for spot cleaning, that can be used between regular baths if necessary. They are not substitutes for regular baths, but they are easy to use for touch-ups as they do not require rinsing.

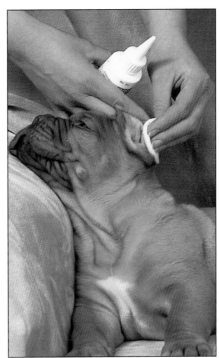

Your Dogue's ears should be checked and cleaned routinely. As you clean the ear with soft cotton and ear solution, be sure the ears are free of mites and any foul odor. *Never* enter the ear canal.

one unintentionally. A long nail also has a better chance of ripping and bleeding, or of causing the feet to spread. If you can hear your dog's nails' clicking on the floor when he walks, his nails are too long.

Before you start cutting, make sure you can identify the "quick" in each nail. The quick is a blood vessel that runs through the center of each nail and grows rather close to the end. It will bleed if accidentally cut, which will be quite painful for the dog as it contains nerve endings. Keep some type of clotting agent on hand, such as a styptic pencil or styptic powder (the type used for shaving). This will stop the bleeding quickly when applied to the end of the cut nail. Do not panic if you cut the

PEDICURE TIP

A dog that spends a lot of time outside on a hard surface, such as cement or pavement, will have his nails naturally worn down and may not need to have them trimmed as often, except maybe in the colder months when he is not outside as much. Regardless, it is best to get your dog accustomed to the nail-trimming procedure at an early age so that he is used to it. Some dogs are especially sensitive about having their feet touched, but if a dog has experienced it since puppyhood, it should not bother him.

Nail Maintenance

Nail Casing

Quick

Cut Line

Dark-Colored Nails

With black or dark nails, it's best to clip only the tip of the nail or to use a file.

Light-Colored Nails

In light-colored nails, clipping is much simpler because you can see the vein (or quick) that grows inside the casing.

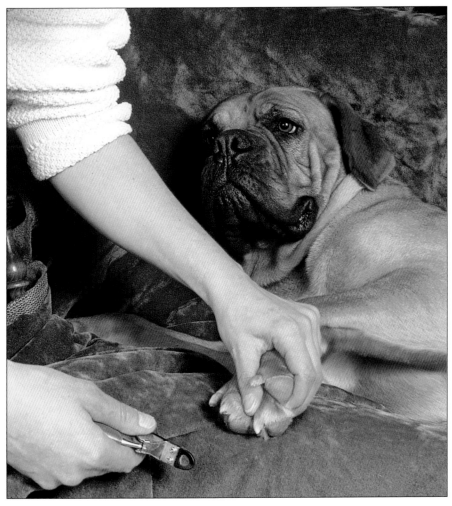

Clipping your dog's nails doesn't have to be an unpleasant experience. Usually dogs who have had their nails clipped since puppyhood are tolerant of the experience.

quick, just stop the bleeding and talk soothingly to your dog. Once he has calmed down, move on to the next nail. It is better to clip a little at a time, particularly with black-nailed dogs.

Hold your pup steady as you begin trimming his nails; you do not want him to make any sudden movements or run away. Talk to him soothingly and stroke him as you clip. Hold his foot in your hand and simply take off the end of each nail in one quick clip. Nail clippers that are specially made for dogs can usually be found wherever you buy pet or grooming supplies.

TRAVELING WITH YOUR DOG
CAR TRAVEL

You should accustom your Dogue de Bordeaux to riding in a car at an early age. You may or may not often take him in the car, but he will need to go to the vet and you do not want these trips to be traumatic for the dog or a big hassle for you. The safest way for a dog to ride in the car is in his crate provided your vehicle can accommodate your Dogue's large crate.

Never allow your Dogue to travel in your car without being restrained. A crate will help keep your dog safe while traveling.

Put the pup in the crate and see how he reacts. If he seems uneasy, you can have a passenger hold him on his lap while you drive. Another option is a specially made safety harness for dogs, which straps the dog in much like a seat belt, or, if you have a station wagon, sports utility or similar vehicle, you can partition the rear section to create an area of safe confinement. Regardless, do not let the dog roam loose in the vehicle—this is

very dangerous! If you should stop short, your dog can be thrown and injured. If the dog starts climbing on you and pestering you while you are driving, you will not be able to concentrate on the road. It is an unsafe situation for everyone—human and canine.

For long trips, be prepared to stop to let the dog relieve himself. Bring along whatever you need to clean up after him. You should take along some paper towels and perhaps some old rags for use should he have a potty accident in the car or suffer from motion sickness.

AIR TRAVEL

Contact your chosen airline before proceeding with travel plans that include your Dogue. The dog will be required to travel in a fiberglass crate and you should always check in advance with the airline regarding specific requirements for the crate's size, type and labeling, as well as any travel restrictions and health certification.

To help put the dog at ease, give him one of his favorite toys in the crate. Do not feed the dog for several hours prior to checking in so that you minimize his need to relieve himself. Some airlines require you to provide documentation as to when the dog has last been fed. In any case, a light meal is best. For long trips, you will have to attach food and water bowls to the dog's crate so that airline employees can tend to him between legs of the trip.

Make sure that your dog is properly identified and that your contact information appears on his ID tags and on his crate. Animals travel in a different area of the plane than human passengers, so every rule must be strictly

Your selection of a suitable boarding kennel should be based on location, cleanliness, the staff's knowledge, cost and activities for your Dogue.

do not want to reserve a place for your family without mentioning that you are taking a dog, because, if it is against the hotel's policy,

COLLAR REQUIRED

If your dog gets lost, he is not able to ask for directions home. Identification tags fastened to the collar give important information—the dog's name, the owner's name, the owner's address and a telephone number where the owner can be reached. This makes it easy for whoever finds the dog to contact the owner and arrange to have the dog returned. An added advantage is that a person will be more likely to approach a lost dog who has ID tags on his collar; it tells the person that this is somebody's pet rather than a stray. This is the easiest and fastest method of identification, provided that the tags stay on the collar and the collar stays on the dog.

Although your Dogue is perfectly able to protect himself, it is the owner's responsibility to ensure his safety, in the form of proper identification, vaccinations and protection from possible poisons or toxins.

followed so as to prevent the risk of getting separated from your dog.

VACATIONS AND BOARDING

So you want to take a family vacation—and you want to include *all* members of the family. You would probably make arrangements for accommodations ahead of time anyway, but this is especially important when traveling with a dog. You do not want to make an overnight stop at the only place around for miles and discover that they do not allow dogs. Also, you

you end up without a place to stay.

Alternatively, if you are traveling and choose not to bring your Dogue de Bordeaux, you will have to make arrangements for him while you are away. Some options are to bring him to a friend's house to stay while you are gone, to have a trusted neighbor stop by often or stay at your house or to bring your dog to a reputable boarding kennel. If you choose to board him at a kennel, you should visit in advance to see the facility and where the dogs are kept. Talk to some of the employees and see how they treat the dogs—do they spend time with the dogs, play with them, exercise them, etc.? Also find out the kennel's policy on vaccinations and what they require. This is for the safety of all the dogs. When dogs are kept together, there is a greater risk of diseases being passed from dog to dog.

IDENTIFICATION

Your Dogue de Bordeaux is your valued companion and friend. That is why you always keep a close eye on him and you have made sure that he cannot escape from the yard or wriggle out of his collar and run away from you. However, accidents can happen and there may come a time when your dog unexpectedly gets separated from you. If this unfortunate event should occur, the first thing on your mind will be finding him. Proper identification will increase the chances of his being returned to you safely and quickly.

IDENTIFICATION OPTIONS

As puppies become more and more expensive, especially those puppies of high quality for showing and/or breeding, they have a greater chance of being stolen. The usual collar dog tag is, of course, easily removed. But there are two more permanent techniques that have become widely used for identification.

The puppy microchip implantation involves the injection of a small microchip, about the size of a corn kernel, under the skin of the dog. If your dog shows up at a clinic or shelter, or is offered for resale under less-than-savory circumstances, it can be positively identified by the microchip. The microchip is scanned, and a registry quickly identifies you as the owner.

Tattooing is done on various parts of the dog, from his belly to his ears. The number tattooed can be your telephone number or any other number that you can easily memorize. When professional dog thieves see a tattooed dog, they usually lose interest. For the safety of our dogs, no laboratory facility or dog broker will accept a tattooed dog as stock. Both microchipping and tattooing can be done at your local veterinary clinic.

TRAINING YOUR
Dogue de Bordeaux

Living with an untrained dog is a lot like owning a piano that you do not know how to play—it is a nice object to look at, but it does not do much more than that to bring you pleasure. Now try taking piano lessons, and suddenly the piano comes alive and brings forth magical sounds and rhythms that set your heart singing and your body swaying.

The same is true with your Dogue de Bordeaux. At first you enjoy seeing him around the house. He does not do much with you other than need food, water and exercise. Come to think of it, he does not bring you much joy, either. He is a big responsibility with a very small return. He may develop unacceptable behaviors that annoy you, to say nothing of

REAP THE REWARDS
If you start with a normal, healthy dog and give him time, patience and some carefully executed lessons, you will reap the rewards of that training for the life of the dog. And what a life it will be! The two of you will find immeasurable pleasure in the companionship you have built together with love, respect and understanding.

bad habits that may end up costing you great sums of money. Not a good thing!

Now train your Dogue de Bordeaux. Enroll in an obedience class. Teach him good manners as you learn how and why he behaves the way he does. Find out how to communicate with your dog and how to recognize and understand his communications with you. Suddenly the dog takes on a new role in your life—he is smart, interesting, well behaved and fun to be with. He demonstrates his bond of devotion to you daily. Your Dogue de Bordeaux does wonders for your ego because he constantly reminds you that you are not only his leader, you are his hero! Miraculous things have happened—you have a wonderful dog (even your family and friends have noticed the transformation!) and you feel good about yourself.

Those involved with teaching dog obedience and counseling owners about their dogs' behavior have discovered some interesting facts about dog ownership. For example, training dogs when they are puppies results in the highest rate of success in developing well-

Dogs gain much information through their acute sense of smell; this is how they find their relief area time and again.

mannered and well-adjusted adult dogs. Training an older dog, from six months to six years of age, can produce almost equal results, providing that the owner accepts the dog's slower rate of learning capability and is willing to work patiently to help the dog succeed at developing to his fullest potential. Unfortunately, many owners of untrained adult dogs lack the patience factor and do not persist until their dogs are successful at learning particular behaviors.

Training a puppy aged 10 to 16 weeks (20 weeks at the most) is like working with a dry sponge in a pool of water. The pup soaks up whatever you show him and constantly looks for more things to do and learn. At this early age, his body is not yet producing hormones, and therein lies the reason for such a high rate of success. Without hormones, he is

PARENTAL GUIDANCE

Training a dog is a life experience. Many parents admit that much of what they know about raising children they learned from caring for their dogs. Dogs respond to love, fairness and guidance, just as children do. Become a good dog owner and you may become an even better parent.

focused on his owners and not particularly interested in investigating other places, dogs, people, etc. You are his leader: his provider of food, water, shelter and security. Therefore, he latches onto you and wants to stay close. He will usually follow you from room to room, will not let you out of his sight when you are outdoors with him and will respond in like manner to the people and animals you encounter. If you greet a friend warmly, he will be happy to greet the person as well. If, however, you are hesitant or anxious about the approach of a stranger, he will respond according to you.

Once the puppy begins to produce hormones, his natural curiosity emerges and he begins to investigate the world around him. It is at that time when you may notice that the untrained dog begins to wander away from you and even ignore your commands

to stay close. When this behavior becomes a problem, there is no option except to train the dog!

Occasionally there will be no classes available within a reasonable distance from your home. Sometimes there are classes available but the tuition is too costly. Whatever the circumstances, the solution to training your Dogue without formal obedience classes lies within the pages of this book. You can do much to train your dog yourself. This chapter is devoted to helping you train your Dogue de Bordeaux at home. If the recommended procedures are

MEALTIME

Mealtime should be a peaceful time for your puppy. Do not put his food and water bowls in a high-traffic area in the house. For example, give him his own little corner of the kitchen where he can eat undisturbed and where he will not be underfoot. Do not allow small children or other family members to disturb the pup when he is eating.

followed faithfully, you may expect positive results that will prove rewarding to both you and your dog.

Whether your Dogue de Bordeaux is a puppy or a mature adult, the methods of teaching and the techniques we use in training basic behaviors are the same. After all, no dog, whether puppy or adult, likes harsh or inhumane methods. All creatures, however, respond favorably to gentle motivational methods and sincere praise and encouragement. Now let us get started.

HOUSEBREAKING

You can train a puppy to relieve himself wherever you choose, but this must be somewhere suitable. You should bear in mind from the outset that when your puppy is old enough to go out in public places, any canine deposits must be removed at once. You will always have to carry with you a small plastic bag or "poop scoop." City dwellers often train their puppies to relieve themselves along the curbside because large plots of grass are not readily available. Suburbanites, on the other hand, usually have yards to accommodate their dogs' needs.

Outdoor training includes such surfaces as grass, soil and cement. Indoor training usually means training your dog to newspaper—not a viable option for Dogue owners. When deciding on

the surface and location that you will want your Dogue de Bordeaux to use, be sure it is going to be permanent. Training your dog to grass and then changing your mind two months later is extremely difficult for both dog and owner.

Next, choose the command you will use each and every time you want your puppy to void. "Go hurry up" and "Go make" are examples of commands commonly used by dog owners. Get in the habit of giving the puppy your chosen relief command before you take him out. That way, when he becomes an adult, you will be able to determine if he wants to go out when you ask him. A confirmation will be signs of interest, such as wagging his tail, watching you intently, going to the door, etc.

PUPPY'S NEEDS
Your puppy needs to relieve himself after play periods, after each meal, after he has been

CALM DOWN
Dogs will do anything for your attention. If you reward the dog when he is calm and attentive, you will develop a well-mannered dog. If, on the other hand, you greet your dog excitedly and encourage him to wrestle with you, the dog will greet you the same way and you will have a hyperactive dog on your hands.

sleeping and any time he indicates that he is looking for a place to urinate or defecate. The urinary and intestinal tract muscles of very young puppies are not fully developed. Therefore, like human babies, puppies need to relieve themselves frequently.

Take your puppy out often—every hour for an eight-week-old, for example, and always immedi-

HOW MANY TIMES A DAY?

AGE	RELIEF TRIPS
To 14 weeks	10
14–22 weeks	8
22–32 weeks	6
Adulthood (dog stops growing)	4

These are estimates, of course, but they are a guide to the *minimum* number of opportunities a dog should have each day to relieve himself.

ately after feeding or sleeping. The older the puppy, the less often he will need to relieve himself. Finally, as a mature healthy adult, he will require only three to five relief trips per day.

HOUSING

Since the types of housing and control you provide for your puppy have a direct relationship on the success of house-training, we consider the various aspects of

both before we begin training. Bringing a new puppy home and turning him loose in your house can be compared to turning a child loose in an amusement park and telling the child that the place is all his! The sheer enormity of the place would be too much for him to handle.

Instead, offer the puppy clearly defined areas where he can play, sleep, eat and live. A room of the house where the family gathers is the most obvious choice. Puppies are social animals and need to feel a part of the pack right from the start. Hearing your voice, watching you while you are doing things and smelling you nearby are all positive reinforcers that he is now a member of your pack. Usually a family room, the kitchen or a nearby adjoining breakfast area is ideal for providing safety and security for both puppy and owner.

Within that room, there should be a smaller area that the puppy can call his own. An alcove, a wire or fiberglass dog crate or a partitioned (not boarded!) corner from which he can view the activities of his new family will be fine. The size of the area or crate is the key factor here. The area must be large enough for the puppy to lie down and stretch out as well as stand up without rubbing his head on the top, yet small enough so that he cannot relieve himself at one

Canine Development Schedule

It is important to understand how and at what age a puppy develops into adulthood. If you are a puppy owner, consult the following Canine Development Schedule to determine the stage of development your Dogue de Bordeaux puppy is currently experiencing. This knowledge will help you as you work with the puppy in the weeks and months ahead.

Period	Age	Characteristics
First to Third	**Birth to Seven Weeks**	Puppy needs food, sleep and warmth, and responds to simple and gentle touching. Needs mother for security and disciplining. Needs littermates for learning and interacting with other dogs. Pup learns to function within a pack and learns pack order of dominance. Begin socializing with adults and children for short periods. Begins to become aware of his environment.
Fourth	**Eight to Twelve Weeks**	Brain is fully developed. Needs socializing with outside world. Remove from mother and littermates. Needs to change from canine pack to human pack. Human dominance necessary. Fear period occurs between 8 and 16 weeks. Avoid fright and pain.
Fifth	**Thirteen to Sixteen Weeks**	Training and formal obedience should begin. Less association with other dogs, more with people, places, situations. Period will pass easily if you remember this is pup's change-to-adolescence time. Be firm and fair. Flight instinct prominent. Permissiveness and over-disciplining can do permanent damage. Praise for good behavior.
Juvenile	**Four to Eight Months**	Another fear period about 7 to 8 months of age. It passes quickly, but be cautious of fright and pain. Sexual maturity reached. Dominant traits established. Dog should understand sit, down, come and stay by now.

Note: These are approximate time frames. Allow for individual differences in puppies.

From house-breaking to basic commands to teaching manners, you shape your puppy's behavior from the moment you bring him home.

end and sleep at the other without coming into contact with his droppings. Dogs are, by nature, clean animals and will not remain close to their relief areas unless forced to do so. In those cases,

HONOR AND OBEY

Dogs are the most honorable animals in existence. They consider another species (humans) as their own. They interface with you. You are their leader. Puppies perceive children to be on their level; their actions around small children are different from their behavior around their adult masters.

they become dirty dogs and usually remain that way for life.

The crate or area should be lined with a clean bedding and offer one toy, no more. Do not put food or water in the crate, as eating and drinking will activate the puppy's digestive processes and ultimately defeat your purpose, as well as make the puppy very uncomfortable as he attempts to hold it.

CONTROL

By *control*, we mean helping the puppy to create a lifestyle pattern that will be compatible to that of his human pack (you!). Just as we guide little children to learn our way of life, we must show the puppy when it is time to play, eat, sleep, exercise and even entertain himself.

Your puppy should always sleep in his crate. He should also learn that, during times of household confusion and excessive human activity such as at breakfast when family members are preparing for the day, he can play by himself in relative safety and comfort in his crate.

Each time you leave the puppy alone, he should be crated. Puppies are chewers. They cannot tell the difference between lamp cords, television wires, shoes, table legs, etc. Chewing into a television wire can be fatal to the puppy, while a shorted wire can start a fire in the house.

If the puppy chews on the arm of the chair when he is alone, you will probably discipline him angrily when you get home. Thus, he makes the association that your coming home means he is going to be punished. (He will not remember chewing up the chair and is incapable of making the association of the discipline with his naughty deed.) Accustoming the pup to his crate not only keeps him safe but also prevents him from engaging in destructive behaviors when you are not there to supervise.

Times of excitement, such as family parties, visits, etc., can be fun for the puppy, providing he can view the activities from the security of his crate. He is not underfoot and he is not being fed all sorts of tidbits that will probably cause him stomach distress, yet he still feels a part of the fun.

SCHEDULE
A puppy should be taken to his relief area each time he is released from his crate, after meals, after play sessions, when he first awakens in the morning (at eight weeks old, this can mean 5 am!) and whenever he indicates by circling or sniffing busily that he needs to urinate or defecate. For a puppy less than ten weeks of age, a routine of taking him out every hour is necessary. As the puppy grows, he will be able to wait for longer periods of time.

Housing is a big part of training your dog. Your Dogue will not want to soil where he sleeps and will usually need to relieve himself after spending a period of time in his crate.

Keep trips to his relief area short. Stay no more than five or six minutes and then return to the house. If he goes during that time, praise him lavishly and take him indoors immediately. If he does not, but he has an accident when you go back indoors, pick him up immediately, say "No! No!" and return to his relief area. Wait a few minutes, then return to the house again. *Never* hit a puppy or put his face in urine or excrement when he has an accident!

PAPER CAPER
Never line your pup's sleeping area with newspaper. Puppy litters are usually raised on newspaper and, once in your home, the puppy will immediately associate newspaper with voiding. Never put newspaper on any floor while house-training, as this will only confuse the puppy. Finally, restrict water intake after evening meals. Offer a few licks at a time—never let a young puppy (or adult) gulp water after meals or at any time.

Puppy's digestive systems are gentle and must be treated as such. Like young babies, pups have very little control of their excretory functions (and are pretty sloppy eaters, too).

Once indoors, put the puppy in his crate until you have had time to clean up his accident. Then release him to the family area and watch him more closely than before. Chances are, his accident was a

Purchase equipment for cleaning up after your dog. The easier it is for you, the more likely you are to do it!

THE CLEAN LIFE

By providing sleeping and resting quarters that fit the dog, and offering frequent opportunities to relieve himself outside his quarters, the puppy quickly learns that the outdoors is the place to go when he needs to urinate or defecate. It also reinforces his innate desire to keep his sleeping quarters clean. This, in turn, helps develop the muscle control that will eventually produce a dog with clean living habits.

result of your not picking up his signal or waiting too long before offering him the opportunity to relieve himself.

Let the puppy learn that going outdoors means it is time to relieve himself, not play. Once trained, he will be able to play indoors and out and still differentiate between the times for play versus the times for relief.

Help him develop regular hours for naps, being alone, playing by himself and just resting, all in his crate. Encourage the pup to entertain himself while you are busy with your activities. Let him learn that having you near is comforting, but it is not your main purpose in life to provide him with undivided attention.

Each time you put your puppy in his crate, tell him "Crate time!" (or whatever command you choose). Soon, he will run to his crate when he hears you say those words.

In the beginning of his training, do not leave him in his crate for prolonged periods of time except during the night when everyone is sleeping. Make his experience with his crate a pleasant one and, as an adult, he will love his crate and willingly stay in it for several hours. There are millions of people who go to work every day and leave their adult dogs crated while they are away. The dogs accept this as their lifestyle and look forward to "crate time."

Training your Dogue de Bordeaux should be taken very seriously. An untrained dog, especially one of this size, can cause quite a bit of trouble.

Crate training provides safety for you, the puppy and the home. It also provides the puppy with a feeling of security, and that helps the puppy achieve self-confidence and clean habits. Remember that one of the primary ingredients in house-training your puppy is control. Regardless of your

TAKE THE LEAD

Do not carry your dog to his relief area. Lead him there on a leash or, better yet, encourage him to follow you to the spot. If you start carrying him to his spot, you might end up doing this routine forever and your dog will have the satisfaction of having trained *you*.

THE SUCCESS METHOD
6 Steps to Successful Crate Training

1 Tell the puppy "Crate time!" and place him in the crate with a small treat (a piece of cheese or half of a biscuit). Let him stay in the crate for five minutes while you are in the same room. Then release him and praise lavishly. Never release him when he is fussing. Wait until he is quiet before you let him out.

2 Repeat Step 1 several times a day.

3 The next day, place the puppy in the crate as before. Let him stay there for ten minutes. Do this several times.

4 Continue building time in five-minute increments until the puppy stays in his crate for 30 minutes with you in the room. Always take him to his relief area after prolonged periods in his crate.

5 Now go back to Step 1 and let the puppy stay in his crate for five minutes, this time while you are out of the room.

6 Once again, build crate time in five-minute increments with you out of the room. When the puppy will stay willingly in his crate (he may even fall asleep!) for 30 minutes with you out of the room, he will be ready to stay in it for several hours at a time.

lifestyle, there will always be occasions when you will need to have a place where your dog can stay and be happy and safe. Crate training is the answer for now and the future.

In conclusion, a few key elements are really all you need for a successful house-training method—consistency, frequency, praise, control and supervision. By following these procedures with a normal, healthy puppy, you and the puppy will soon be past the stage of accidents and ready to move on to a clean and rewarding life together.

ROLES OF DISCIPLINE, REWARD AND PUNISHMENT

Discipline, training one to act in accordance with rules, brings order to life. It is as simple as that. Without discipline, particularly in a group society, chaos reigns supreme and the group will eventually perish. Humans and canines are social animals and need some form of discipline in order to function effectively. They must procure food, reproduce to keep their species going and protect their home base and their young. If there were no discipline in the lives of social animals, they

Dr. Edward Thorndike, a noted psychologist, established *Thorndike's Theory of Learning,* which states that a behavior that results in a pleasant event tends to be repeated. Likewise, a behavior that results in an unpleasant event tends not to be repeated. Today's training methods are based on this theory. For example, if you manipulate a dog to perform a specific behavior and reward him for doing it, he is likely to do it again because he enjoyed the end result.

Occasionally, punishment, a penalty inflicted for an offense, is necessary. The best type of punishment often comes from an outside source. For example, a child is told not to touch the stove because he may get burned. He disobeys and touches the stove. In doing so, he receives a burn. From that time on, he respects the heat of the stove and avoids contact with it. Therefore,

Your house-trained Dogue will let you know when he needs to go out...listen to him! Full-grown dogs should be able to control their urges for about six hours at a time, usually longer during the night.

would eventually die from starvation and/or predation by other stronger animals. In the case of domestic canines, dogs need discipline in their lives in order to understand how their pack (you and other family members) functions and how they must act in order to survive.

A large humane society in a highly populated area recently surveyed dog owners regarding their satisfaction with their relationships with their dogs. People who had trained their dogs were 75% more satisfied with their pets than those who had never trained their dogs.

KEEP SMILING

Never train your dog, puppy or adult, when you are angry or in a sour mood. Dogs are very sensitive to human feelings, especially anger, and if your dog senses that you are angry or upset, he will connect your anger with his training and learn to resent or fear his training sessions.

a behavior that results in an unpleasant event tends not to be repeated.

A good example of a dog learning the hard way is the dog that chases the house cat. He is told many times to leave the cat alone, yet he persists in teasing the cat. Then, one day he begins chasing the cat, but the cat turns and swipes a claw across the dog's face, leaving him with a painful gash on his nose. The final result is that the dog stops chasing the cat.

TRAINING EQUIPMENT
COLLAR
A simple buckle collar is fine for most dogs. One who pulls mightily on the leash may require a choke collar for training.

LEAD
A 1- to 2-yard lead is recommended, preferably made of leather, nylon or heavy cloth. A chain lead is not recommended, as many dog owners find that the chain cuts into their hands and that switching the lead back and forth frequently between their hands is painful.

TREATS
Have a bag of treats on hand. Something nutritious and easy to swallow works best; use a soft treat, a chunk of cheese or a piece of cooked chicken rather than a dry biscuit. By the time

---

PLAN TO PLAY

The puppy should also have regular play and exercise sessions when he is with you or a family member. Exercise for a very young puppy can consist of a short walk around the house or yard. Playing can include fetching games with a large ball or a special toy. (All puppies teethe and need soft things upon which to chew.) Remember to restrict play periods to indoors within his living area (the family room, for example) until he is completely house-trained.

---

the dog gets done chewing a dry treat, he will forget why he is being rewarded in the first place! Using food rewards will not teach a dog to beg at the table—the only way to teach a dog to beg at the table is to give him food from the table. In training, rewarding the dog with a food treat will help him associate praise and the treats with learning new behaviors that obviously please his owner.

TRAINING BEGINS: ASK THE DOG A QUESTION
In order to teach your dog, you must first get his attention. He cannot learn anything if he is looking away from you with his mind on something else.

To get his attention, ask him "School?" and immediately walk over to him and give him a treat as you tell him "Good dog." Wait a minute or two and repeat the routine, this time with a treat in your hand as you approach within a foot of the dog. Do not go directly to him, but stop about a foot away and hold out the treat as you ask "School?" He will see you approaching with a treat in your hand and most likely begin walking toward you. As you meet, give him the treat and praise again.

The third time, ask the question, have a treat in your hand and walk only a short distance toward the dog so that he must walk almost all the way to you. As he reaches you, give him the treat and praise again.

By this time, the dog will probably be getting the idea that if he pays attention to you, espe-

cially when you ask that question, it will pay off in treats and fun activities for him. In other words, he learns that "school" means doing fun things with you that result in treats and positive attention for him.

Remember that the dog does not understand your verbal language, he only recognizes sounds. Your question translates to a series of sounds for him, and those sounds become the signal to go to you and pay attention. If he does, he will get to interact with you plus receive treats and praise.

THE BASIC COMMANDS
TEACHING SIT

Now that you have the dog's attention, hold the lead in your left hand and the food treat in your right. Place your food hand at the dog's nose and let him lick the treat but not take it from you. Say "Sit" and slowly raise your

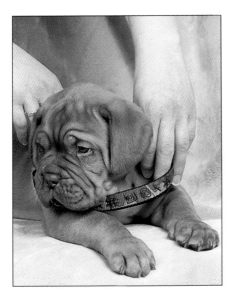

A simple buckle collar is sufficient for your Dogue puppy. Identification tags should be attached to his collar.

TRAINING RULES

If you want to be successful in training your dog, you have four rules to obey yourself:
1. Develop an understanding of how a dog thinks.
2. Do not blame the dog for lack of communication.
3. Define your dog's personality and act accordingly.
4. Have patience and be consistent.

food hand from in front of the dog's nose up over his head so that he is looking at the ceiling. As he bends his head upward, he will have to bend his knees to maintain his balance. As he bends his knees, he will assume a sit position. At that point, release the food treat and praise lavishly with comments such as "Good dog! Good sit!" Always remember to praise enthusiastically. Dogs relish verbal praise from their owners and feel so proud of themselves whenever they accomplish a behavior.

You will not use food forever in getting the dog to obey your commands. Food is only used to teach new behaviors, and once the dog knows what you want when you give a specific command, you will wean him off the food treats but maintain the verbal praise. After all, you will always have your voice with you, but there will be many times when you have no food rewards yet expect the dog to obey.

COMMAND STANCE

Stand up straight and authoritatively when giving your dog commands. Do not issue commands when lying on the floor or lying on your back on the sofa. If you are on your hands and knees when you give a command, your dog will think you are positioning yourself to play.

TEACHING DOWN

Teaching the down exercise is easy when you understand how the dog perceives the down position, and it is very difficult when you do not. Dogs perceive the down position as a submissive posture. In addition, teaching the down exercise using the wrong method can sometimes make the dog develop such a fear of the down that he either runs away when you say "Down" or attempts to snap at the person who tries to force him down.

Have the dog sit close alongside your left leg, facing in the same direction as you are. Hold the lead in your left hand and a food treat in your right. Now place your left hand lightly on the top of the dog's shoulders where they meet above the spinal cord. Do not push down on the dog's shoulders; simply rest your left hand there so you can guide the dog to lie down close to your left leg rather than to swing away from your side when he drops.

Now place the food hand at the dog's nose, say "Down" very softly (almost a whisper) and slowly lower the food hand to the dog's front feet. When the food hand reaches the floor, begin moving it forward along the floor in front of the dog. Keep talking softly to the dog, saying things like, "Do you want this treat? You can do this, good dog." Your reas-

Again, we use food and praise during the teaching process as we help the dog to understand exactly what it is that we are expecting him to do.

To teach the sit/stay, start with the dog sitting on your left side as before and hold the lead in your left hand. Have a food treat in your right hand and place your food hand at the dog's nose. Say "Stay" and step out on your right foot to stand directly in front of the dog, toe to toe, as he licks and nibbles the treat. Be sure to keep his head facing upward to maintain the sit position. Count to five and then swing around to stand next to the dog again with him on your left. As soon as

It is much easier to teach a Dogue puppy than a full-grown Dogue. Not only do pups learn faster but it is also very difficult physically to guide a dog of this size into the desired positions.

suring tone of voice will help calm the dog as he tries to follow the food hand in order to get the treat.

When the dog's elbows touch the floor, release the food and praise softly. Try to get the dog to maintain that down position for several seconds before you let him sit up again. The goal here is to get the dog to settle down and not feel threatened in the down position.

TEACHING STAY
It is easy to teach the dog to stay in either a sit or a down position.

LANGUAGE BARRIER
Dogs do not understand our language and have to rely on tone of voice more than just words or sound. They can be trained to react to a certain sound, at a certain volume. If you say "No, Oliver" in a very soft, pleasant voice, it will not have the same meaning as "No, Oliver!!" when you raise your voice. You should never use the dog's name during a reprimand, just the command "No! " You never want the dog to associate his name with a negative experience or reprimand.

you get back to the original position, release the food and praise lavishly.

To teach the down/stay, do the down as previously described. As soon as the dog lies down, say "Stay" and step out on your right foot just as you did in the sit/stay.

DOUBLE JEOPARDY

A dog in jeopardy never lies down. He stays alert on his feet because instinct tells him that he may have to run away or fight for his survival. Therefore, if a dog feels threatened or anxious, he will not lie down. Consequently, it is important to keep the dog calm and relaxed as he learns the down exercise.

Count to five and then return to stand beside the dog with him on your left side. Release the treat and praise as always.

Within a week or ten days, you can begin to add a bit of distance between you and your dog when you leave him. When you do, use your left hand open with the palm facing the dog as a stay signal, much the same as the hand signal a police officer uses to stop traffic at an intersection. Hold the food treat in your right hand as before, but this time the food is not touching the dog's nose. He will watch the food hand and quickly learn that he is going to get that treat as soon as you return to his side.

When you can stand 3 feet away from your dog for 30 seconds, you can then begin building time and distance in both stays. Eventually, the dog can be expected to remain in the stay position for prolonged periods of time until you return to him or call him to you. Always praise lavishly when he stays.

TEACHING COME

If you make teaching "come" a fun experience, you should never have a student that does not love the game or that fails to come when called. The secret, it seems, is never to teach the word "come."

At times when an owner most wants his dog to come when called, the owner is likely upset or anxious and he allows these feelings to come through in the tone of his voice when he calls his dog. Hearing that desperation in his owner's voice, the dog fears the results of going to him and therefore either disobeys or runs in the opposite direction. The secret, therefore, is to teach the dog a game and, when you want him to come to you, simply play the game. It is practically a no-fail solution!

To begin, have several members of your family take a few food treats and each go into a different room in the house. Take turns calling the dog. Each person should celebrate the dog's finding him with a treat and lots of happy praise. When a person calls the

It is not difficult to teach your Dogue to stay when he understands what is expected of him. Practice makes perfect.

dog, he is actually inviting the dog to find him and get a treat as a reward for "winning."

A few turns of the "Where are you?" game and the dog will figure out that everyone is playing the game and that each person has a big celebration awaiting the dog's success at locating him. Once the dog learns to love the game, simply calling out "Where are you?" will bring him running from wherever he is when he hears that all-important question.

The come command is recognized as one of the most impor-

PRACTICE MAKES PERFECT!

- Have training lessons with your dog every day in several short segments—three to five times a day for a few minutes at a time is ideal.
- Do not have long practice sessions. The dog will become easily bored.
- Never practice when you are tired, ill, worried or in an otherwise negative mood. This will transmit to the dog and may have an adverse effect on his performance.

Think fun, short and above all *positive*! End each session on a high note, rather than a failed exercise, and make sure to give a lot of praise. Enjoy the training and help your dog enjoy it, too.

tant things to teach a dog, so it is interesting to note that there are trainers who work with thousands of dogs and never teach the actual word "come." Yet these dogs will race to respond to a person who uses the dog's name followed by "Where are you?" In one instance, a woman had a 12-year-old companion dog who went blind, but who never failed to locate her owner when asked "Where are you?"

Children particularly love to play this game with their dogs. Children can hide in smaller places like a shower or bathtub, behind a bed or under a table. The dog needs to work a little bit harder to find these hiding places,

> ### "COME" . . . BACK
> Never call your dog to come to you for a correction or scold him when he reaches you. That is the quickest way to turn a "Come" command into "Go away fast!" Dogs think only in the present tense, and your dog will connect the scolding with coming to you, not with the misbehavior of a few moments earlier.

but, when he does, he loves to celebrate with a treat and a tussle with a favorite youngster.

TEACHING HEEL

Heeling means that the dog walks beside the owner without pulling. It takes time and patience on the owner's part to succeed at teaching the dog that he (the owner) will not proceed unless the dog is walking calmly beside him. Pulling out ahead on the lead is definitely not acceptable.

Begin with holding the lead in your left hand as the dog sits beside your left leg. Hold the loop end of the lead in your right hand but keep your left hand short on the lead so it keeps the dog in close next to you. Say "Heel" and step forward on your left foot. Keep the dog close to you and take three steps. Stop and have the dog sit next to you in what we now call the heel position. Praise verbally, but do not touch the dog. Hesitate a moment and begin

A well-trained Dogue will sit/stay, but he will be eagerly awaiting your OK signal.

again with "Heel," taking three steps and stopping, at which point the dog is told to sit again.

Your goal here is to have the dog walk those three steps without pulling on the lead. When he will walk calmly beside you for three steps without pulling, increase the number of steps you take to five. When he will walk politely beside you while you take five steps, you can increase the length of your walk to ten steps. Keep increasing the length of your stroll until the dog will walk quietly beside you without pulling as long as you want him to heel. When you stop heeling, indicate to the dog that the exercise is over by verbally praising as you pet him and say "OK, good dog." The "OK" is used as a release word, meaning that the exercise is finished and the dog is free to relax.

If you are dealing with a dog who insists on pulling you around, simply "put on your

How about a handshake...or a "pawshake"? Training doesn't always have to be serious. Dogues can be taught to do fun things too!

brakes" and stand your ground until the dog realizes that the two of you are not going anywhere until he is beside you and moving at your pace, not his. It may take some time just standing there to convince the dog that you are the leader and you will be the one to decide on the direction and speed of your travel.

Each time the dog looks up at you or slows down to give a slack lead between the two of you, quietly praise him and say "Good heel. Good dog." Eventually, the dog will begin to respond and within a few days he will be walking politely beside you with-

---

"WHERE ARE YOU?"

When calling the dog, do not say "Come." Say things like, "Rover, where are you? See if you can find me! I have a biscuit for you!" Keep up a constant line of chatter with coaxing sounds and frequent questions such as, "Where are you?" The dog will learn to follow the sound of your voice to locate you and receive his reward.

Heel is not just a necessary command for the show ring. Every Dogue must learn to walk politely on the lead for every-day walks.

TUG OF WALK?
If you begin teaching the heel by taking long walks and letting the dog pull you along, he misinterprets this action as an acceptable form of taking a walk. When you pull back on the lead to counteract his pulling, he reads that tug as a signal to pull even harder!

out pulling on the lead. At first, the training sessions should be kept short and very positive; soon the dog will be able to walk nicely with you for increasingly longer distances. Remember also to give the dog free time and the opportunity to run and play when you are done with heel practice.

WEANING OFF FOOD IN TRAINING

Food is used in training new behaviors, yet once the dog understands what behavior goes with a specific command, it is time to start weaning him off the food treats. At first, give a treat after each exercise. Then, start to give a treat only after every other exercise. Mix up the times when you offer a food reward and the times when you only offer praise so that the dog will never know when he is going to receive both food and praise and when he is going to receive only praise. This is called a variable-ratio reward system and it proves successful because there is always the chance that the owner will produce a treat, so the dog never stops trying for that reward. No matter what, *always* give verbal praise.

OBEDIENCE CLASSES

As previously discussed, it is a good idea to enroll in an obedience class if one is available in your area. Many areas have dog clubs that offer basic obedience training as well as preparatory classes for obedience competition. There are also local dog trainers who offer similar classes.

At obedience trials, dogs can earn titles at various levels of competition. The beginning levels of competition include basic behaviors such as sit, down, heel, etc. The more advanced levels of competition include jumping, retrieving, scent discrimination and signal work. The advanced levels require a dog and owner to put a lot of time and effort into their training, and the titles that can be earned at these levels of competition are very prestigious.

OTHER ACTIVITIES FOR LIFE

Whether a dog is trained in the structured environment of a class or alone with his owner at home, there are many activities that can bring fun and rewards to both owner and dog once they have mastered basic control.

Teaching the dog to help out around the home, in the yard or on the farm provides great satisfaction to both dog and owner. In addition, the dog's help makes life a little easier for his owner and raises his stature as a valued companion to his family. It helps give the dog a purpose; it helps to keep his mind occupied and provides an outlet for his energy.

Backpacking is an exciting and healthy activity that the dog can be taught without assistance

HEELING WELL
Teach your dog to heel in an enclosed area. Once you think the dog will obey reliably and you want to attempt advanced obedience exercises such as off-lead heeling, test him in a fenced-in area so he cannot run away.

Within the Dogue de Bordeaux lies much ability and potential. Give him the opportunity to develop to his fullest through proper training and exposure to a range of activities.

from more than his owner. The exercise of walking and climbing is good for man and dog alike, and the bond that they develop together is priceless. The rule of thumb is to never allow the dog to carry more than one-sixth of his body weight.

If you are interested in participating in organized competition with your Dogue de Bordeaux, there are activities other than obedience in which you and your dog can become involved. Agility is a popular and fun sport where dogs run through an obstacle course that includes various jumps, tunnels and other exercises to test the dog's speed and coordination. The owners run through the

course beside their dogs to give commands and to guide them through the course. Although competitive, the focus is on fun—it's fun to do and fun to watch, and great exercise.

OBEDIENCE SCHOOL

A basic obedience beginner's class usually lasts for six to eight weeks. Dog and owner attend an hour-long lesson once a week and practice for a few minutes, several times a day, each day at home. If done properly, the whole procedure will result in a well-mannered dog and an owner who delights in living with a pet that is eager to please and enjoys doing things with his owner.

As a Dogue de Bordeaux owner, you have the opportunity to participate in Schutzhund competition if you choose. Schutzhund originated as a test to determine the best-quality German Shepherds to be used for breeding stock. Now it is open to other breeds, and it is used as a way to evaluate working ability and temperament. There are three levels of Schutzhund: SchH. I, SchH. II and SchH. III. Each level consists of training, obedience and protection phases and are progressively more difficult to complete successfully. Training for Schutzhund is intense and must be practiced consistently to keep the dog keen. The experience of Schutzhund training is very

A BORN PRODIGY

Occasionally, a dog and owner who have not attended formal classes have been able to earn entry-level titles by obtaining competition rules and regulations from a local kennel club and practicing on their own to a degree of perfection. Obtaining the higher level titles, however, almost always requires extensive training under the tutelage of experienced instructors. In addition, the more difficult levels require more specialized equipment whereas the lower levels do not.

rewarding for dog and owner, and the Dogue de Bordeaux's tractability is well suited for this type of training, which should be done with the help of a professional.

Although the Dogue is not a typical agility-trial contender, with proper training and precautions, the breed can excel in this venue as well.

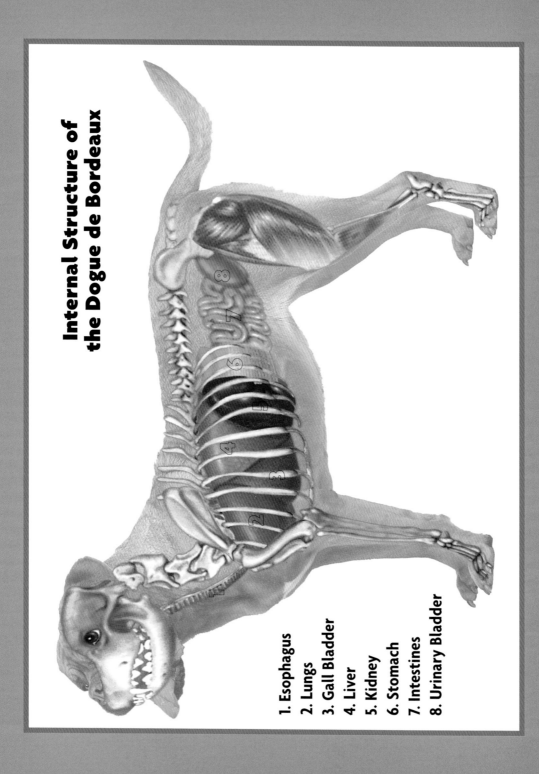

Internal Structure of the Dogue de Bordeaux

1. Esophagus
2. Lungs
3. Gall Bladder
4. Liver
5. Kidney
6. Stomach
7. Intestines
8. Urinary Bladder

Dogue de Bordeaux

Dogs, being mammals like human beings, suffer from many of the same physical illnesses as people. They might even share many of the psychological problems. Since people usually know more about human diseases than canine maladies, many of the terms used in this chapter will be the familiar terms, not necessarily those used by veterinarians. We'll use the term *x-ray*, instead of the more acceptable term *radiograph*. We will also use the familiar term *symptoms* even though dogs don't have symptoms, which are verbal descriptions of the patient's feelings; dogs have *clinical signs*. Since dogs can't speak, we have to look for clinical signs...but we will use the term *symptoms* in this book.

As a general rule, medicine is *practiced*. That term is not arbitrary. Medicine is a constantly changing art as we learn more and more about genetics, electronic aids (like CAT scans and MRI scans) and new findings. There are many dog maladies, like canine hip dysplasia, that are not universally treated in the same manner. For example, some vets opt for surgery more often than others do.

SELECTING A QUALIFIED VETERINARIAN

Your selection of a veterinarian should be based not only upon personality and ability with dogs, especially with large-breed dogs, but also upon his convenience to your home. You want a vet who is close, as you might have emergencies or require multiple visits for treatments. You want a vet who has services that you might require such as a boarding facilities and tattooing, and of course who has a good reputation for ability and responsiveness. There is nothing more frustrating than having to wait to get a response from your veterinarian.

Before you buy your Dogue de Bordeaux, meet and interview the veterinarians in your area. Take everything into consideration; discuss background, specialties, fees, emergency policy, etc.

Breakdown of Veterinary Income by Category

2%	Dentistry
4%	Radiology
12%	Surgery
15%	Vaccinations
19%	Laboratory
23%	Examinations
25%	Medicines

A typical vet's income, categorized according to services performed. This survey dealt with small-animal (pets) practices.

All vets are licensed and should be capable of dealing with routine health issues such as injuries, infections, routine surgeries (stitching up wounds, neutering/spaying, etc.) and the promotion of health (for example, by vaccination). There are, however, many veterinary specialties that require further studies and internships. For example, there are specialists in heart problems (veterinary cardiologists), skin problems (veterinary dermatologists), teeth and gum problems (veterinary dentists), eye problems (veterinary ophthalmologists) and x-rays (veterinary radiologists), and surgeons who have specialties in bones, muscles or certain organs.

When the problem affecting your dog is serious, your vet will refer you to a specialist in the appropriate field. It is not unusual or impudent to get another medical opinion, although it is courteous to advise the vets concerned about this. You might also want to compare costs between several veterinarians. Sophisticated health care and veterinary services can be very costly. Don't be bashful about discussing these costs with your veterinarian or his staff. It is not infrequent that important decisions are based upon financial considerations.

PREVENTATIVE MEDICINE

It is much easier, less costly and more effective to practice preventative medicine than to fight bouts of illness and disease. Properly bred puppies come from parents that were selected based upon their genetic-disease profiles. Their mother should have been vaccinated, free of all internal and external parasites and properly nourished. The dam can pass on disease resistance to her puppies, which can last for eight to ten weeks. She can also pass on parasites and many infections. That's why it is helpful to know as much about the dam's health as you possibly can.

WEANING TO GOING TO NEW HOMES

Puppies should be weaned by the time they are about six to eight weeks old. A puppy that remains for at least eight weeks with his

First Aid at a Glance

Burns
Place the affected area under cool water; use ice if only a small area is burnt.

Bee stings/Insect bites
Apply ice to relieve swelling; antihistamine dosed properly.

Animal bites
Clean any bleeding area; apply pressure until bleeding subsides; go to the vet.

Spider bites
Use cold compress and a pressurized pack to inhibit venom's spreading.

Antifreeze poisoning
Immediately induce vomiting by using hydrogen peroxide.

Fish hooks
Removal best handled by vet; hook must be cut in order to remove.

Snake bites
Pack ice around bite; contact vet quickly; identify snake for proper antivenin.

Car accident
Move dog from roadway with blanket; seek veterinary aid.

Shock
Calm the dog; keep him warm; seek immediate veterinary help.

Nosebleed
Apply cold compress to the nose; apply pressure to any visible abrasion.

Bleeding
Apply pressure above the area; treat wound by applying a cotton pack.

Heat stroke
Submerge dog in cold bath; cool down with fresh air and water; go to the vet.

Frostbite/Hypothermia
Warm the dog with a warm bath, electric blankets or hot water bottles.

Abrasions
Clean the wound and wash out thoroughly with fresh water; apply antiseptic.

 Remember: an injured dog may attempt to bite a helping hand from fear and confusion. Always muzzle the dog before trying to offer assistance.

mother and littermates usually adapts better to other dogs and people later in life.

Many people have their newly acquired puppy examined by a veterinarian immediately, which is good idea. The puppy will have his teeth examined, his skeletal conformation checked and his general health evaluated prior to certification by the veterinarian. Puppies sometimes have problems with their kneecaps, cataracts and other eye problems, heart murmurs and undescended testicles. Your vet might also have training in temperament evaluation. At the first visit, the vet will set up your pup's vaccination schedule.

Vaccination Scheduling
Vaccination programs usually begin when the puppy is very young. Some vets give a first vaccination at six to eight weeks, though some breeders prefer the course to commence at eight to ten weeks so as not interfere with the dam's passing of antibodies. Most vaccinations are given by injection and should only be done by a veterinarian. Both he and you should keep a record of the date of the injection, the identification of the vaccine and the amount given. Vaccinations are usually based on a two-to four-week cycle. You must take your vet's advice as to when to vaccinate, as this may differ according to the vaccine used.

Most vaccinations immunize your puppy against viruses. The usual vaccines contain immunizing doses of several different viruses such as distemper, parvovirus, parainfluenza and hepatitis. There are other vaccines available when the puppy is at risk. You should rely upon professional advice. This is especially true for the booster-shot program. Most vaccination programs require a booster when the puppy is one year old, and once a year thereafter. In some cases, circumstances may require more or less frequent immunizations.

Canine cough, more formally known as tracheobronchitis, is treated with a vaccine that is sprayed into the dog's nostrils. Your veterinarian will explain and manage all of these details.

DEWORMING
Caring for the puppy starts before the puppy is born by keeping the dam healthy and well-nourished. Most puppies have worms, even if they are not evident, so a worming program is essential. The worms continually shed eggs except during their dormant stage, when they just rest in the tissues of the puppy. During this stage they are not evident during a routine examination.

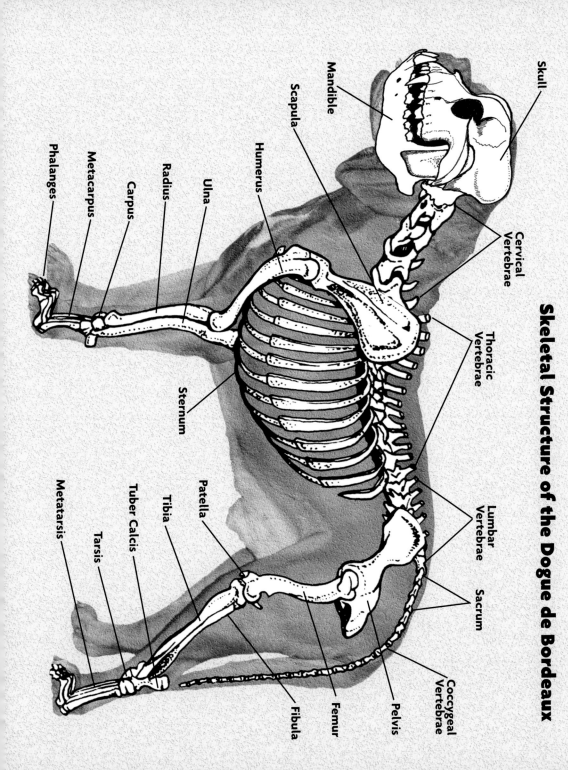

Skeletal Structure of the Dogue de Bordeaux

- Skull
- Mandible
- Scapula
- Cervical Vertebrae
- Thoracic Vertebrae
- Humerus
- Radius
- Ulna
- Carpus
- Metacarpus
- Phalanges
- Sternum
- Lumbar Vertebrae
- Sacrum
- Coccygeal Vertebrae
- Pelvis
- Femur
- Fibula
- Patella
- Tibia
- Tuber Calcis
- Tarsis
- Metatarsis

HEALTH AND VACCINATION SCHEDULE

Age in Weeks:	3rd	6th	8th	10th	12th	14th	16th	20-24th
Worm Control	✔	✔	✔	✔	✔	✔	✔	✔
Neutering								✔
Heartworm		✔						✔
Parvovirus		✔		✔		✔		✔
Distemper			✔		✔		✔	
Hepatitis			✔		✔		✔	
Leptospirosis		✔		✔		✔		
Parainfluenza		✔		✔		✔		
Dental Examination			✔					✔
Complete Physical			✔					✔
Temperament Testing			✔					
Coronavirus					✔			
Canine Cough		✔						
Hip Dysplasia							✔	
Rabies								✔

Vaccinations are not instantly effective. It takes about two weeks for the dog's immune system to develop antibodies. Most vaccinations require annual booster shots. Your veterinarian should guide you in this regard.

FIVE MONTHS TO ONE YEAR OF AGE
By the time your puppy is five months old, he should have completed his vaccination program. During his physical examination he should be evaluated for the common hip dysplasia and other diseases of the joints. There are tests to assist in the prediction of these problems, as well as tests that can be run to assess the effectiveness of the vaccination program.

Unless you intend to breed or show your dog, neutering the puppy around six months of age is recommended. Discuss this with your veterinarian; most professionals advise neutering puppy. Neutering and spaying have proven to be extremely beneficial to both male and female dogs, respectively. Besides eliminating the possibility of pregnancy and pyometra in females and testicular cancer in males, it greatly reduces the risk of (but does not prevent) breast cancer in bitches and prostate cancer in male dogs.

Blood tests are performed for heartworm infestation and it is possible that your puppy will be placed on a preventative therapy that will prevent heartworm infection as well as control other internal parasites. A complete dental examination should also be performed.

Dogs Older than One Year

Continue to visit the veterinarian at least once a year. There is no such disease as old age, but bodily functions do change with age. The eyes and ears are no longer as efficient, nor are the internal workings of the liver, kidneys and intestines. Proper dietary changes, recommended by your veterinarian, can make life more pleasant for the aging Dogue de Bordeaux and you.

VACCINE ALLERGIES
Vaccines do not work all the time. Sometimes dogs are allergic to them and many times the antibodies, which are supposed to be stimulated by the vaccine, just are not produced. You should keep your dog in the veterinary clinic for an hour after he is vaccinated to be sure there are no allergic reactions.

SKIN PROBLEMS IN DOGUES DE BORDEAUX

Veterinarians are consulted by dog owners for skin problems more than for any other group of diseases or maladies. Dogs' skin is

Disease	What is it?	What causes it?	Symptoms
Leptospirosis	Severe disease that affects the internal organs; can be spread to people.	A bacterium, which is often carried by rodents, that enters through mucous membranes and spreads quickly throughout the body.	Range from fever, vomiting and loss of appetite in less severe cases to shock, irreversible kidney damage and possibly death in most severe cases.
Rabies	Potentially deadly virus that infects warm-blooded mammals.	Bite from a carrier of the virus, mainly wild animals.	1st stage: dog exhibits change in behavior, fear. 2nd stage: dog's behavior becomes more aggressive. 3rd stage: loss of coordination, trouble with bodily functions.
Parvovirus	Highly contagious virus, potentially deadly.	Ingestion of the virus, which is usually spread through the feces of infected dogs.	Most common: severe diarrhea. Also vomiting, fatigue, lack of appetite.
Canine cough	Contagious respiratory infection.	Combination of types of bacteria and virus. Most common: *Bordetella bronchiseptica* bacteria and parainfluenza virus.	Chronic cough.
Distemper	Disease primarily affecting respiratory and nervous system.	Virus that is related to the human measles virus.	Mild symptoms such as fever, lack of appetite and mucus secretion progress to evidence of brain damage, "hard pad."
Hepatitis	Virus primarily affecting the liver.	Canine adenovirus type I (CAV-1). Enters system when dog breathes in particles.	Lesser symptoms include listlessness, diarrhea, vomiting. More severe symptoms include "blue-eye" (clumps of virus in eye).
Coronavirus	Virus resulting in digestive problems.	Virus is spread through infected dog's feces.	Stomach upset evidenced by lack of appetite, vomiting, diarrhea.

Your Dogue is completely unaware of possible allergens and toxins in the great outdoors. You must keep his safety in mind whenever exposing him to areas that are unfamiliar to you.

almost as sensitive as human skin and both suffer almost the same ailments (though the occurrence of acne in most breeds is rare). For this reason, veterinary dermatology has developed into a specialty practiced by many vets.

Since many skin problems have visual symptoms that are almost identical, it requires the skill of an experienced veterinary dermatologist to identify and cure many of the more severe skin disorders. Pet shops sell many treatments for skin problems, but

most are directed at symptoms and not the underlying problem(s). If your dog is suffering from a skin disorder, seek professional assistance as quickly as possible. The earlier a disease is identified and treated, the more likely it is that the cure will be successful.

HEREDITARY SKIN DISORDERS
Veterinary dermatologists are currently researching a number of skin disorders that are believed to have hereditary bases. These inherited diseases are transmitted by both parents, who appear (phenotypically) normal but have a recessive gene for the disease, meaning that they carry, but are not affected by, the disease. These diseases pose serious problems to breeders because in some instances there are no methods of identifying carriers. Often the secondary diseases associated with these skin conditions are even more debilitating than the skin disorders themselves, including cancers and respiratory problems.

Among the hereditary skin disorders, for which the mode of inheritance is known, are acrodermatitis, cutaneous asthenia (Ehlers-Danlos syndrome), sebaceous adenitis, cyclic hematopoiesis, dermatomyositis, IgA deficiency, color dilution alopecia and nodular dermatofibrosis. Some of these disorders are limited to one or two breeds, while others affect a large number of breeds. All inherited diseases must be diagnosed and treated by a veterinary specialist.

AUTO-IMMUNE SKIN CONDITIONS

Auto-immune skin conditions are commonly referred to as being allergic to yourself. Allergies, though, usually result in inflammatory reactions to an outside stimulus. Auto-immune diseases cause serious damage to the tissues involved.

The best known auto-immune disease is lupus. It affects people as well as dogs. The symptoms are very variable and may affect the kidneys, bones, blood chemistry and skin. It can be fatal to both dogs and humans, though it is not thought to be transmissible. It is usually successfully treated with cortisone, prednisone or similar corticosteroid, but extensive use of these drugs can have harmful side effects.

ACRAL LICK GRANULOMA

Dogues de Bordeaux and many other dogs have a very poorly understood syndrome called acral lick granuloma. The manifestation of the problem is the dog's tireless attack at a specific area of the body, almost always the legs. The dog licks so intensively that he removes the hair and skin, leaving an ugly, large wound. There is no absolute cure, but corticosteroids are the most common treatment.

DENTAL HEALTH

A dental examination is in order when the dog is between six months and one year of age so that any permanent teeth that have erupted incorrectly can be corrected. It is important to begin a tooth-brushing routine at home, using dental-care products designed for dogs. Durable nylon and safe edible chews should be a part of your puppy's arsenal for good health, good teeth and pleasant breath. The vast majority of dogs three to four years old and older has diseases of the gums from lack of dental attention. Using the various types of dental chews can be very effective in controlling dental plaque.

PARASITE BITES

Many of us are allergic to mosquito bites. The bites itch, erupt and may even become infected. Dogs have the same reaction to fleas, ticks and/or mites. When you feel the prick of the mosquito as it bites you, you have a chance to kill it with your hand. Unfortunately, when your dog is bitten by a flea, tick or mite, he can only scratch it away or bite it. By the time the dog has been bitten, the parasite has done some of its damage. It may also have laid eggs to cause further problems in the near future. The itching from parasite bites is probably due to the saliva injected into the site when the parasite sucks the dog's blood.

SIMULATED MEDICAL CONDITION FOR EDUCATIONAL PURPOSES ONLY.

Many large breeds of dog are prone to acral lick syndrome. The dog will lick at a spot, usually on one of his front legs, until he has removed all the hair and much of the skin. Your veterinarian can treat the problem, but the cause and the cure are not known.

AIRBORNE ALLERGIES

Just as humans have hay fever, rose fever and other fevers from which they suffer during the pollinating season, many dogs suffer from the same allergies. When the pollen count is high, your dog might suffer, but don't expect him to sneeze and have a runny nose as humans would. Dogs react to pollen allergies the same way they react to fleas—they scratch and bite themselves. Dogues de Bordeaux are very susceptible to airborne pollen allergies.

Dogs, like humans, can be tested for allergens. Discuss the testing with your veterinary dermatologist.

FOOD PROBLEMS

FOOD ALLERGIES

Dogs are allergic to many foods that are best-sellers and highly recommended by breeders and veterinarians. Changing the brand of food that you buy may not eliminate the problem because the element of the food to which the dog is allergic may also be contained in the new brand.

Recognizing a food allergy is difficult. Humans vomit or have rashes when they eat a food to which they are allergic. Dogs neither vomit nor (usually) develop a rash. Instead they itch, scratch and bite, thus making the diagnosis extremely difficult. While pollen allergies and para-site bites are usually seasonal, food allergies are year-round problems.

FOOD INTOLERANCE

Food intolerance is the inability of the dog to completely digest certain foods. For example, puppies that may have done very well on their mother's milk may

THE PROTEIN QUESTION
Your dog's protein needs are change-able. High activity level, stress, climate and other physical factors may require your dog to have more protein in his diet. Check with your veterinarian.

not do well on cow's milk. Food intolerance may cause loose bowels, passage of gas and stomach pains. These are the only obvious symptoms of food intolerance and that makes diagnosis difficult, since these symptoms are often common to other problems as well.

TREATING FOOD PROBLEMS
Handling food allergies and food intolerance yourself is possible. Put your dog on a diet that he has never had. Obviously, if he has never eaten this new food, he can't yet have been allergic or intolerant of it. Start with a single ingredient that is *not* in the dog's diet at the present time. Ingredients like chopped beef or chicken are common in dog's diets, so try something like fish, lamb or another quality protein source. Keep the dog on this diet (with no additives) for a month. If the symptoms of food allergy or intolerance disappear, chances are that you have defined the cause.

Don't think that the single ingredient cured the problem. You still must find a suitable diet and ascertain which ingredient in the old diet was objectionable. This is most easily done by adding ingredients to the new diet one at a time until the problem is solved. Let the dog stay on the modified diet for a month before you add another ingredient.

HOW TO PREVENT BLOAT
Research has confirmed that the structure of deep-chested breeds contributes to their predisposition to bloat. Nevertheless, there are several precautions that you can take to reduce the risk of this condition:
- Feed your dog twice daily rather than offer one big meal.
- Do not exercise your dog for at least one hour before and two hours after he has eaten.
- Make certain that your dog is calm and not overly excited while he is eating. It has been proven that nervous or overly excited dogs are more prone to develop bloat.
- Add a small portion of moist meat product to his dry food ration.
- Serve his meals in an elevated bowl stand, which avoids the dog's craning his neck while eating.
- To prevent your dog from gobbling his food too quickly, and thereby swallowing air, put some large (unswallowable) toys into his bowl so that he will have to eat around them to get his food.

An alternative method is to study the ingredients in the diet to which your dog is allergic or intolerable. Identify the main ingredient in this diet and eliminate it by buying a different food that does not have that ingredient. Keep experimenting until the symptoms disappear after one month on the new diet.

A male dog flea, *Ctenocephalides canis.*

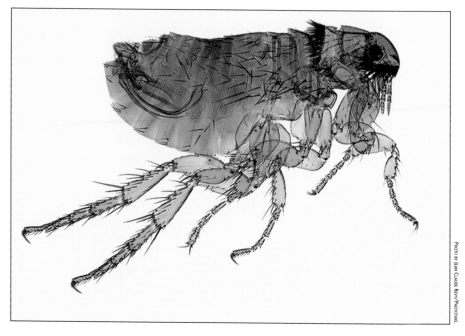

EXTERNAL PARASITES
FLEAS

Of all the problems to which dogs are prone, none is more well known and frustrating than fleas. Flea infestation is relatively simple to cure but difficult to prevent. Parasites that are harbored inside the body are a bit more difficult to eradicate but they are easier to control.

To control flea infestation, you have to understand the flea's life cycle. Fleas are often thought of as a summertime problem, but centrally heated homes have changed the patterns and fleas can be found at any time of the year. The most effective method of flea control is a two-stage approach: one stage to kill the adult fleas, and the other to control the development of pre-adult fleas. Unfortunately, no single active ingredient is effective against all stages of the life cycle.

FLEA KILLER CAUTION—"POISON"

Flea-killers are poisonous. You should not spray these toxic chemicals on areas of a dog's body that he licks, including his genitals and his face. Flea killers taken internally are a better answer, but check with your vet in case internal therapy is not advised for your dog.

LIFE CYCLE STAGES

During its life, a flea will pass through four life stages: egg, larva, pupa or nymph and adult. The adult stage is the most visible and irritating stage of the flea life cycle, and this is why the majority of flea-control products concentrate on this stage. The fact is that adult fleas account for only 1% of the total flea population, and the other 99% exist in pre-adult stages, i.e., eggs, larvae and nymphs. The pre-adult stages are barely visible to the naked eye.

THE LIFE CYCLE OF THE FLEA

Eggs are laid on the dog, usually in quantities of about 20 or 30, several times a day. The adult female flea must have a blood meal before each egg-laying session. When first laid, the eggs will cling to the dog's hair, as the eggs are still moist. However, they will quickly dry out and fall from the dog, especially if the dog moves around or scratches. Many eggs will fall off in the dog's favorite area or an area in which he spends a lot of time, such as his bed.

Once the eggs fall from the dog onto the carpet or furniture, they will hatch into larvae. This takes from one to ten days. Larvae are not particularly mobile and will usually travel only a few inches from where they hatch. However, they do have a tendency to move away from bright light and heavy

EN GARDE:
CATCHING FLEAS OFF GUARD!
Consider the following ways to arm yourself against fleas:
- Add a small amount of pennyroyal or eucalyptus oil to your dog's bath. These natural remedies repel fleas.
- Supplement your dog's food with fresh garlic (minced or grated) and a hearty amount of brewer's yeast, both of which ward off fleas.
- Use a flea comb on your dog daily. Submerge fleas in a cup of bleach to kill them quickly.
- Confine the dog to only a few rooms to limit the spread of fleas in the home.
- Vacuum daily...and get all of the crevices! Dispose of the bag every few days until the problem is under control.
- Wash your dog's bedding daily. Cover cushions where your dog sleeps with towels, and wash the towels often.

traffic—under furniture and behind doors are common places to find high quantities of flea larvae.

The flea larvae feed on dead organic matter, including adult flea feces, until they are ready to change into adult fleas. Fleas will usually remain as larvae for around seven days. After this period, the larvae will pupate into protective pupae. While inside the pupae, the larvae will undergo

Fleas have been measured as being able to jump 300,000 times and can jump 150 times their length in any direction, including straight up.

metamorphosis and change into adult fleas. This can take as little time as a few days, but the adult fleas can remain inside the pupae waiting to hatch for up to two years. The pupae are signaled to hatch by certain stimuli, such as physical pressure—the pupae's being stepped on, heat from an animal's lying on the pupae or increased carbon-dioxide levels and vibrations—indicating that a suitable host is available.

Once hatched, the adult flea must feed within a few days. Once the adult flea finds a host, it will not leave voluntarily. It only becomes dislodged by grooming or the host animal's scratching.

PHOTO BY DWIGHT R. KUHN

The adult flea will remain on the host for the duration of its life unless forcibly removed.

TREATING THE ENVIRONMENT AND THE DOG

Treating fleas should be a two-pronged attack. First, the environment needs to be treated; this includes carpets and furniture, especially the dog's bedding and areas underneath furniture. The environment should be treated with a household spray containing an Insect Growth Regulator (IGR) and an insecticide to kill the adult fleas. Most IGRs are effective against eggs and larvae; they actually mimic the fleas' own hormones and stop the eggs and larvae from developing into adult fleas. There are currently no treatments available to attack the pupa stage of the life cycle, so the adult insecticide is used to kill the newly hatched adult fleas before they find a host. Most IGRs are active for many months, while

A scanning electron micrograph of a dog or cat flea, *Ctenocephalides,* magnified more than 100x. This image has been colorized for effect.

S. E. M. BY DR DENNIS KUNKEL, UNIVERSITY OF HAWAII

THE LIFE CYCLE OF THE FLEA

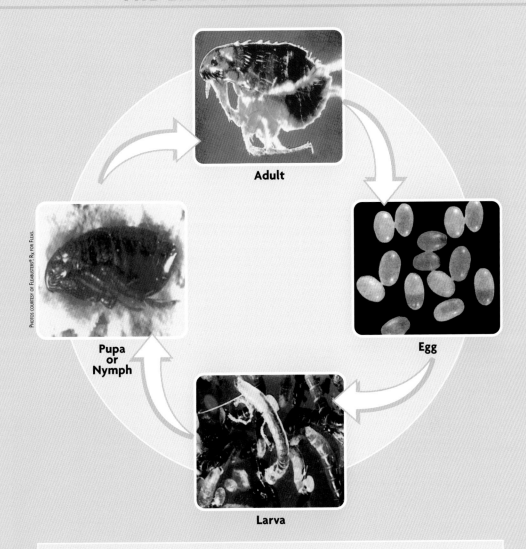

Adult

Egg

Larva

Pupa
or
Nymph

Fleas have been around for millions of years and have adapted to changing host animals. They are able to go through a complete life cycle in less than one month or they can extend their lives to almost two years by remaining as pupae or cocoons. They do not need blood or any other food for up to 20 months.

> ## INSECT GROWTH REGULATOR (IGR)
>
> Two types of products should be used when treating fleas—a product to treat the pet and a product to treat the home. Adult fleas represent less than 1% of the flea population. The pre-adult fleas (eggs, larvae and pupae) represent more than 99% of the flea population and are found in the environment; it is in the case of pre-adult fleas that products containing an Insect Growth Regulator (IGR) should be used in the home.
>
> IGRs are a new class of compounds used to prevent the development of insects. They do not kill the insect outright, but instead use the insect's biology against it to stop it from completing its growth. Products that contain methoprene are the world's first and leading IGRs. Used to control fleas and other insects, this type of IGR will stop flea larvae from developing and protect the house for up to seven months.

The American dog tick, *Dermacentor variabilis*, is probably the most common tick found on dogs. Look at the strength in its eight legs! No wonder it's hard to detach them.

adult insecticides are only active for a few days.

When treating with a household spray, it is a good idea to vacuum before applying the product. This stimulates as many pupae as possible to hatch into adult fleas. The vacuum cleaner should also be treated with an insecticide to prevent the eggs and larvae that have been collected in the vacuum bag from hatching.

The second stage of treatment is to apply an adult insecticide to the dog. Traditionally, this would be in the form of a collar or a spray, but more recent innovations include digestible insecticides that poison the fleas when they ingest the dog's blood. Alternatively, there are drops that, when placed on the back of the dog's neck, spread throughout the dog's hair and skin to kill adult fleas.

TICKS

Though not as common as fleas, ticks are found all over the tropical and temperate world. They don't bite, like fleas; they harpoon. They dig their sharp proboscis (nose) into the dog's skin and drink the blood. Their

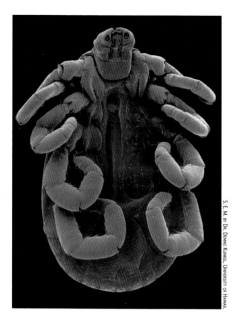

S. E. M. BY DR. DENNIS KUNKEL, UNIVERSITY OF HAWAII

only food and drink is dog's blood. Dogs can get Lyme disease, Rocky Mountain spotted fever, tick bite paralysis and many other diseases from ticks. They may live where fleas are found and they like to hide in cracks or seams in walls. They are controlled the same way fleas are controlled.

The American dog tick, *Dermacentor variabilis*, may well be the most common dog tick in many geographical areas, especially those areas where the climate is hot and humid. Most dog ticks have life expectancies of a week to six months, depending upon climatic conditions. They can neither jump nor fly, but they can crawl slowly and can range up to 16 feet to reach a sleeping or unsuspecting dog.

MITES

Just as fleas and ticks can be problematic for your dog, mites can also lead to an itchy nuisance. Microscopic in size, mites are related to ticks and generally take up permanent residence on their host animal—in this case, your dog! The term *mange* refers to any infestation caused by one of the mighty mites, of which there are six varieties that concern dog owners.

Demodex mites cause a condition known as demodicosis

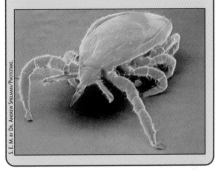

DEER-TICK CROSSING
The great outdoors may be fun for your dog, but it also is home to dangerous ticks. Deer ticks carry a bacterium known as *Borrelia burgdorferi* and are most active in the autumn and spring. When infections are caught early, penicillin and tetracycline are effective antibiotics, but, if left untreated, the bacteria may cause neurological, kidney and cardiac problems as well as long-term trouble with walking and painful joints.

S. E. M. BY DR. ANDREW SPIELMAN/PHOTOTAKE.

PHOTO BY DR. DENNIS KUNKEL, UNIVERSITY OF HAWAII.

The head of an American dog tick, *Dermacentor variabilis*, enlarged and colorized for effect.

The mange mite, *Psoroptes bovis*, can infest cattle and other domestic animals.

Human lice look like dog lice; the two are closely related.

(sometimes called red mange or follicular mange), in which the mites live in the dog's hair follicles and sebaceous glands in larger-than-normal amounts. This type of mange is commonly passed from the dam to her puppies and usually shows up on the puppies' muzzles, though demodicosis is not transferable from one normal dog to another. Most dogs recover from this type of mange without any treatment, though topical therapies are commonly prescribed by the vet.

The *Cheyletiellosis* mite is the hook-mouthed culprit associated with "walking dandruff," a condition that affects dogs as well as cats and rabbits. This mite lives on the surface of the animal's skin and is readily transferable through direct or indirect contact with an affected animal. The dandruff is present in the form of scaly skin, which may or may not be itchy. If not treated, this mange can affect a whole kennel of dogs and can be spread to humans as well.

The *Sarcoptes* mite causes intense itching on the dog in the form of a condition known as scabies or sarcoptic mange. The cycle of the *Sarcoptes* mite lasts about three weeks, and the mites live in the top layer of the dog's skin (epidermis), preferably in areas with little hair. Scabies is highly contagious and can be passed to humans. Sometimes an allergic reaction to the mite worsens the severe itching associated with sarcoptic mange.

Ear mites, *Otodectes cynotis,* lead to otodectic mange, which most commonly affects the outer ear canal of the dog, though other areas can be affected as well. Dogs with ear-mite infestation commonly scratch at their ears, causing further irritation, and shake their heads. Dark brown droppings in the outer ear confirm the diagnosis. Your vet can prescribe a treatment to flush out the ears and kill any eggs in the ears. A complete month of treatment is necessary to cure the mange.

Two other mites, less common in dogs, include *Dermanyssus gallinae* (the poultry or red mite) and *Eutrombicula alfreddugesi* (the North American mite associated with trombiculidiasis or chigger infestation). The poultry mite frequently lives on chickens, but can transfer to dogs who spend time near farm animals. Chigger infestation affects dogs in the

NOT A DROP TO DRINK
Never allow your dog to swim in polluted water or public areas where water quality can be suspect. Even perfectly clear water can harbor parasites, many of which can cause serious to fatal illnesses in canines. Areas inhabited by water-fowl and other wildlife are especially dangerous.

central US who have exposure to woodlands. The types of mange caused by both of these mites are treatable by veterinarians.

INTERNAL PARASITES
Most animals—fishes, birds and mammals, including dogs and humans—have worms and other parasites that live inside their bodies. According to Dr. Herbert R. Axelrod, the fish pathologist, there are two kinds of parasites: dumb and smart. The smart parasites live in peaceful cooperation with their hosts (symbiosis), while the dumb parasites kill their hosts. Most worm infections are relatively easy to control. If they are not controlled, they weaken the host dog to the point that other medical problems occur, but they do not kill the host as dumb parasites would.

A brown dog tick, *Rhipicephalus sanguineus*, is an uncommon but annoying tick found on dogs.

DO NOT MIX
Never mix parasite-control products without first consulting your vet. Some products can become toxic when combined with others and can cause fatal consequences.

The roundworm *Rhabditis* can infect both dogs and humans.

ROUNDWORMS

Average-size dogs can pass 1,360,000 roundworm eggs every day. For example, if there were only 1 million dogs in the world, the world would be saturated with thousands of tons of dog feces. These feces would contain around 15,000,000,000 roundworm eggs.

Up to 31% of home yards and children's sand boxes in the US contain roundworm eggs.

Flushing dog's feces down the toilet is not a safe practice because the usual sewage treatments do not destroy roundworm eggs.

Infected puppies start shedding roundworm eggs at three weeks of age. They can be infected by their mother's milk.

The roundworm, *Ascaris lumbricoides.*

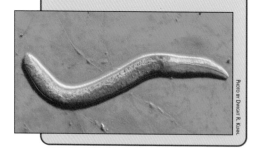

ROUNDWORMS

The roundworms that infect dogs are known scientifically as *Toxocara canis.* They live in the dog's intestines and shed eggs continually. It has been estimated that a dog produces about 6 or more ounces of feces every day. Each ounce of feces averages hundreds of thousands of roundworm eggs. There are no known areas in which dogs roam that do not contain roundworm eggs. The greatest danger of roundworms is that they infect people, too! It is wise to have your dog tested regularly for roundworms.

In young puppies, roundworms cause bloated bellies, diarrhea, coughing and vomiting, and are transmitted from the dam (through blood or milk). Affected puppies will not appear as animated as normal puppies. The worms appear spaghetti-like, measuring as long as 6 inches. Adult dogs can acquire roundworms through coprophagia (eating contaminated feces) or by killing rodents that carry roundworms.

Roundworm infection can kill puppies and cause severe problems in adults, as the hatched larvae travel to the lungs and trachea through the bloodstream. Cleanliness is the best preventative for roundworms. Always pick up after your dog and dispose of feces in appropriate receptacles.

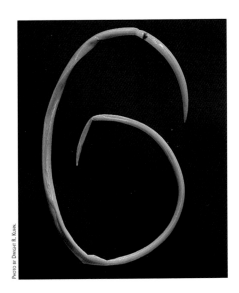

HOOKWORMS

In the United States, dog owners have to be concerned about four different species of hookworm, the most common and most serious of which is *Ancylostoma caninum,* which prefers warm climates. The others are *Ancylostoma braziliense, Ancylostoma tubaeforme* and *Uncinaria stenocephala,* the latter of which is a concern to dogs living in the northern US and Canada, as this species prefers cold climates. Hookworms are dangerous to humans as well as to dogs and cats, and can be the cause of severe anemia due to iron deficiency. The worm uses its teeth to attach itself to the dog's intestines and changes the site of its attachment about six times per day. Each time the worm repositions itself, the dog loses

blood and can become anemic. *Ancylostoma caninum* is the most likely of the four species to cause anemia in the dog.

Symptoms of hookworm infection include dark stools, weight loss, general weakness, pale coloration and anemia, as well as possible skin problems. Fortunately, hookworms are easily purged from the affected dog with a number of medications that have proven effective. Discuss these with your veterinarian. Most heartworm preventatives include a hookworm insecticide as well.

Owners also must be aware that hookworms can infect humans, who can acquire the larvae through exposure to contaminated feces. Since the worms cannot complete their life cycle on a human, the worms simply infest the skin and cause irritation. This condition is known as cutaneous larva migrans syndrome. As a preventative, use disposable gloves or a "poop-scoop" to pick up your dog's droppings and prevent your dog (or neighborhood cats) from defecating in children's play areas.

The hookworm, *Ancylostoma caninum.*

The infective stage of the hookworm larva.

TAPEWORMS

Humans, rats, squirrels, foxes, coyotes, wolves and domestic dogs are all susceptible to tapeworm infection. Except in humans, tapeworms are usually not a fatal infection. Infected individuals can harbor 1000 parasitic worms.

Tapeworms, like some other types of worm, are hermaphroditic, meaning male and female in the same worm.

If dogs eat infected rats or mice, or anything else infected with tapeworm, they get the tapeworm disease. One month after attaching to a dog's intestine, the worm starts shedding eggs. These eggs are infective immediately. Infective eggs can live for a few months without a host animal.

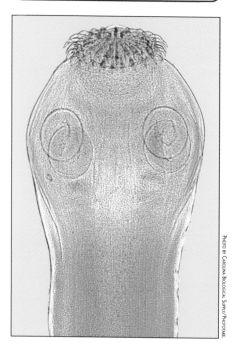

The head and rostellum (the round prominence on the scolex) of a tapeworm, which infects dogs and humans.

PHOTO BY CAROLINA BIOLOGICAL SUPPLY/PHOTOTAKE.

TAPEWORMS

There are many species of tapeworm, all of which are carried by fleas! The most common tapeworm affecting dogs is known as *Dipylidium caninum*. The dog eats the flea and starts the tapeworm cycle. Humans can also be infected with tapeworms—so don't eat fleas! Fleas are so small that your dog could pass them onto your hands, your plate or your food and thus make it possible for you to ingest a flea that is carrying tapeworm eggs.

While tapeworm infection is not life-threatening in dogs (smart parasite!), it can be the cause of a very serious liver disease for humans. About 50% of the humans infected with *Echinococcus multilocularis*, a type of tapeworm that causes alveolar hydatid, perish.

WHIPWORMS

In North America, whipworms are counted among the most common parasitic worms in dogs. The whipworm's scientific name is *Trichuris vulpis*. These worms attach themselves in the lower parts of the intestine, where they feed. Affected dogs may only experience upset tummies, colic and diarrhea. These worms, however, can live for months or years in the dog, beginning their larval stage in the small intestine, spending their adult stage in the large intestine and finally passing infective eggs through the dog's feces. The only way to detect whipworms is through a fecal examination, though this is not always foolproof. Treatment for whipworms is tricky, due to the worms' unusual life-cycle pattern, and very often dogs are reinfected due to exposure to infective eggs on the ground. The whipworm eggs can survive in the environment for as long as five years; thus, cleaning up droppings in your own backyard as well as in public places is absolutely essential for sanitation purposes and the health of your dog and others.

THREADWORMS

Though less common than round-worms, hookworms and those previously mentioned, thread-worms concern dog owners in the southwestern US and Gulf Coast area, where the climate is hot and humid. Living in the small intestine of the dog, this worm measures a mere 2 millimeters and is round in shape. Like that of the whipworm, the threadworm's life cycle is very complex and the eggs and larvae are passed through the feces. A deadly disease in humans, *Strongyloides* readily infects people, and the handling of feces is the most common means of trans-mission. Threadworms are most often seen in young puppies; bloody diarrhea and pneumonia are symptoms. Sick puppies must be isolated and treated immediately; vets recommend a follow-up treat-ment one month later.

HEARTWORM PREVENTATIVES

There are many heartworm preventatives on the market, many of which are sold at your veterinarian's office. These products can be given daily or monthly, depending on the manufacturer's instructions. All of these preventatives contain chemical insecticides directed at killing heartworms, which leads to some controversy among dog owners. In effect, heartworm preventatives are neces-sary evils, though you should determine how necessary based on your pet's lifestyle. There is no doubt that heartworm is a dreadful disease that threatens the lives of dogs. However, the likelihood of your dog's being bitten by an infected mosquito is slim in most places, and a mosquito-repellent (or an herbal remedy such as Wormwood or Black Walnut) is much safer for your dog and will not compromise his immune system (the way heartworm preventatives will). Should you decide to use the tradi-tional preventative "medications," you can consider giving the pill every other or third month. Since the toxins in the pill will kill the heartworms at all stages of develop-ment, the pill would be effective in killing larvae, nymphs or adults, and it takes four months for the larvae to reach the adult stage. Thus, there is no rationale to poison-ing the dog's system on a monthly basis. Lastly, do not give the pill during the winter months since there are no mosquitoes around to pass on their infection, unless you live in a tropical environment.

Life Cycle of the Heartworm

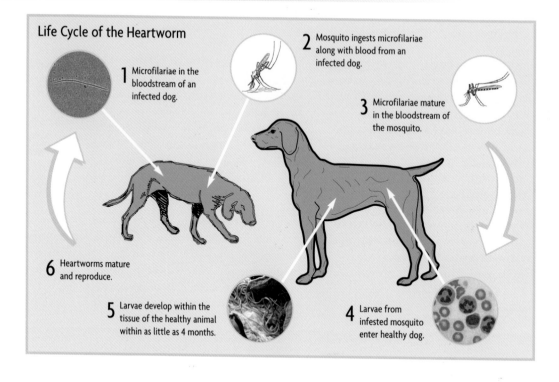

1 Microfilariae in the bloodstream of an infected dog.

2 Mosquito ingests microfilariae along with blood from an infected dog.

3 Microfilariae mature in the bloodstream of the mosquito.

4 Larvae from infested mosquito enter healthy dog.

5 Larvae develop within the tissue of the healthy animal within as little as 4 months.

6 Heartworms mature and reproduce.

HEARTWORMS

Heartworms are thin, extended worms up to 12 inches long, which live in a dog's heart and the major blood vessels surrounding it. Dogs may have up to 200 worms. Symptoms may be loss of energy, loss of appetite, coughing, the development of a pot belly and anemia.

Heartworms are transmitted by mosquitoes. The mosquito drinks the blood of an infected dog and takes in larvae with the blood. The larvae, called microfilariae, develop within the body of the mosquito and are passed on to the next dog bitten after the larvae mature. It takes two to three weeks for the larvae to develop to the infective stage within the body of the mosquito. Dogs are usually treated at about six weeks of age and maintained on a prophylactic dose given monthly.

Blood testing for heartworms is not necessarily indicative of how seriously your dog is infected. Although this is a dangerous disease, it is not easy for a dog to be infected. Discuss the various preventatives with your vet, as there are many different types now available. Together you can decide on a safe course of prevention for your dog.

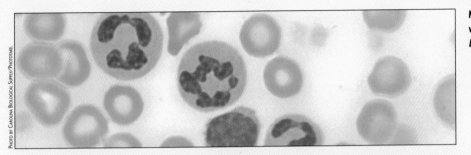

Magnified heart-worm larvae, *Dirofilaria immitis.*

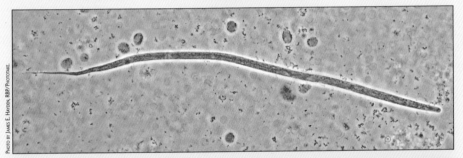

Heartworm, *Dirofilaria immitis.*

The heart of a dog infected with canine heart-worm, *Dirofilaria immitis.*

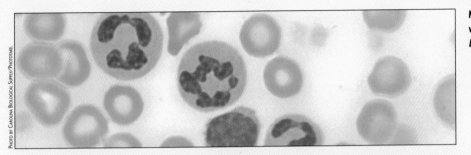

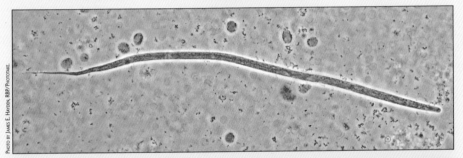

PHOTO BY CAROLINA BIOLOGICAL SUPPLY/PHOTOTAKE.

PHOTO BY JAMES E. HAYDEN, RBP/PHOTOTAKE.

PHOTO BY JAMES E. HAYDEN, RPB/PHOTOTAKE.

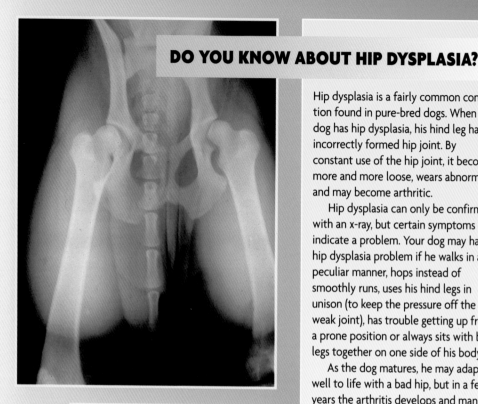

DO YOU KNOW ABOUT HIP DYSPLASIA?

Hip dysplasia is a fairly common condition found in pure-bred dogs. When a dog has hip dysplasia, his hind leg has an incorrectly formed hip joint. By constant use of the hip joint, it becomes more and more loose, wears abnormally and may become arthritic.

Hip dysplasia can only be confirmed with an x-ray, but certain symptoms may indicate a problem. Your dog may have a hip dysplasia problem if he walks in a peculiar manner, hops instead of smoothly runs, uses his hind legs in unison (to keep the pressure off the weak joint), has trouble getting up from a prone position or always sits with both legs together on one side of his body.

As the dog matures, he may adapt well to life with a bad hip, but in a few years the arthritis develops and many dogs with hip dysplasia become crippled.

Hip dysplasia is considered an inherited disease and can usually be diagnosed when the dog is three to nine months old, although a dog is not definitely diagnosed with or certified as clear of the disease until two years of age. Some experts claim that a special diet might help your puppy outgrow the bad hip, but the usual treatments are surgical. The removal of the pectineus muscle, the removal of the round part of the femur, reconstructing the pelvis and replacing the hip with an artificial one are all surgical interventions that are expensive, but they are usually very successful. Follow the advice of your veterinarian.

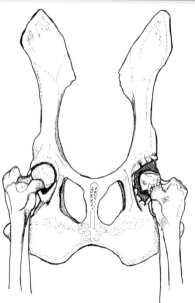

Above: X-ray of dysplastic hips. Hip dysplasia is a badly worn hip joint caused by improper fit of the bone into the socket. It is easily the most common hip problem in Dogues de Bordeaux.
Right: The healthy hip joint on the left and the unhealthy hip joint on the right.

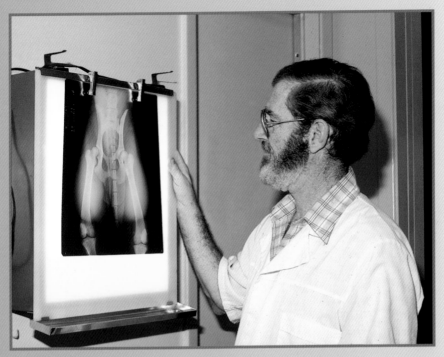

Left: A veterinarian evaluating a dog's x-ray for hip dysplasia. Diagnosis can only be made using radiographic techniques, which are interpreted (read) by a suitably trained veterinarian. Below: X-rays of a dysplastic elbow in a three-and-a-half year-old dog.

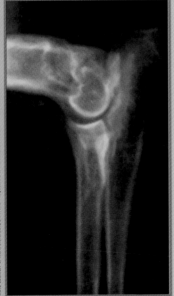

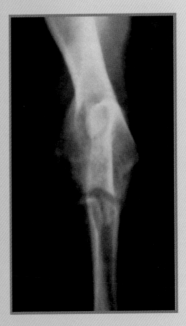

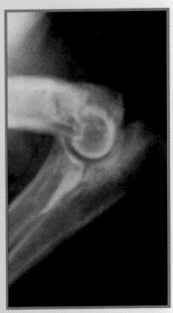

HOMEOPATHY:
an alternative
to conventional
medicine

"Less is Most'"

Using this principle, the strength of a homeopathic remedy is measured by the number of serial dilutions that were undertaken to create it. The greater the number of serial dilutions, the greater the strength of the homeopathic remedy. The potency of a remedy that has been made by making a dilution of 1 part in 100 parts (or 1/100) is 1c or 1cH. If this remedy is subjected to a series of further dilutions, each one being 1/100, a more dilute and stronger remedy is produced. If the remedy is diluted in this way six times, it is called 6c or 6cH. A dilution of 6c is 1 part in 1,000,000,000,000. In general, higher potencies in more frequent doses are better for acute symptoms and lower potencies in more infrequent doses are more useful for chronic, long-standing problems.

CURING YOUR DOG NATURALLY

Holistic medicine means treating the whole animal as a unique, perfect living being. Generally, holistic treatments do not suppress the symptoms that the body naturally produces, as do most medications prescribed by conventional doctors and vets. Holistic methods seek to cure disease by regaining balance and harmony in the patient's environment. Some of these methods include use of nutritional therapy, herbs, flower essences, aromatherapy, acupuncture, massage, chiropractic and, of course the most popular holistic approach, homeopathy.

Homeopathy is a theory or system of treating illness with small doses of substances which, if administered in larger quantities, would produce the symptoms that the patient already has. This approach is often described as "like cures like." Although modern veterinary medicine is geared toward the "quick fix," homeopathy relies on the belief that, given the time, the body is able to heal itself and return to its natural, healthy state.

Choosing a remedy to cure a problem in our dogs is the difficult part of homeopathy. Consult with your veterinarian for a professional diagnosis of your dog's symptoms. Often these symptoms require immediate conventional care. If your vet is willing and knowledgeable, you may attempt a homeopathic remedy. Be aware that cortisone prevents homeopathic remedies from working. There are hundreds of possibilities and combinations to cure many problems in dogs, from basic physical problems such as excessive shedding, fleas or other parasites, unattractive doggy odor, bad breath, upset stomach, obesity, dry, oily or dull coat, diarrhea, ear problems or eye discharge (including tears and dry or mucousy matter), to behavioral abnormalities such as fear of loud noises, habitual licking, poor appetite, excessive barking and various phobias. From alumina to zincum metallicum, the remedies span the planet and the imagination...from flowers and weeds to chemicals, insect droppings, diesel smoke and volcanic ash.

Using "Like to Treat Like"

Unlike conventional medicines that suppress symptoms, homeopathic remedies treat illnesses with small doses of substances that, if administered in larger quantities, would produce the symptoms that the patient already has. While the same homeopathic remedy can be used to treat different symptoms in different dogs, here are some interesting remedies and their uses.

Apis Mellifica
(made from honey bee venom) can be used for allergies or to reduce swelling that occurs in acutely infected kidneys.

Calcarea Fluorica
(made from calcium fluoride, which helps harden bone structure) can be useful in treating hard lumps in tissues.

Diesel Smoke
can be used to help control motion sickness.

Natrum Muriaticum
(made from common salt, sodium chloride) is useful in treating thin, thirsty dogs.

Nitricum Acidum
(made from nitric acid) is used for symptoms you would expect to see from contact with acids, such as lesions, especially where the skin joins the linings of body orifices or openings such as the lips and nostrils.

Symphytum
(made from the herb Knitbone, *Symphytum officinale)* is used to encourage bones to heal.

Urtica Urens
(made from the common stinging nettle) is used in treating painful, irritating rashes.

HOMEOPATHIC REMEDIES FOR YOUR DOG

Symptom/Ailment	Possible Remedy
ALLERGIES	Apis Mellifica 30c, Astacus Fluviatilis 6c, Pulsatilla 30c, Urtica Urens 6c
ALOPECIA	Alumina 30c, Lycopodium 30c, Sepia 30c, Thallium 6c
ANAL GLANDS (BLOCKED)	Hepar Sulphuris Calcareum 30c, Sanicula 6c, Silicea 6c
ARTHRITIS	Rhus Toxicodendron 6c, Bryonia Alba 6c
CATARACT	Calcarea Carbonica 6c, Conium Maculatum 6c, Phosphorus 30c, Silicea 30c
CONSTIPATION	Alumina 6c, Carbo Vegetabilis 30c, Graphites 6c, Nitricum Acidum 30c, Silicea 6c
COUGHING	Aconitum Napellus 6c, Belladonna 30c, Hyoscyamus Niger 30c, Phosphorus 30c
DIARRHEA	Arsenicum Album 30c, Aconitum Napellus 6c, Chamomilla 30c, Mercurius Corrosivus 30c
DRY EYE	Zincum Metallicum 30c
EAR PROBLEMS	Aconitum Napellus 30c, Belladonna 30c, Hepar Sulphuris 30c, Tellurium 30c, Psorinum 200c
EYE PROBLEMS	Borax 6c, Aconitum Napellus 30c, Graphites 6c, Staphysagria 6c, Thuja Occidentalis 30c
GLAUCOMA	Aconitum Napellus 30c, Apis Mellifica 6c, Phosphorus 30c
HEAT STROKE	Belladonna 30c, Gelsemium Sempervirens 30c, Sulphur 30c
HICCOUGHS	Cinchona Deficinalis 6c
HIP DYSPLASIA	Colocynthis 6c, Rhus Toxicodendron 6c, Bryonia Alba 6c
INCONTINENCE	Argentum Nitricum 6c, Causticum 30c, Conium Maculatum 30c, Pulsatilla 30c, Sepia 30c
INSECT BITES	Apis Mellifica 30c, Cantharis 30c, Hypericum Perforatum 6c, Urtica Urens 30c
ITCHING	Alumina 30c, Arsenicum Album 30c, Carbo Vegetabilis 30c, Hypericum Perforatum 6c, Mezerium 6c, Sulphur 30c
KENNEL COUGH	Drosera 6c, Ipecacuanha 30c
MASTITIS	Apis Mellifica 30c, Belladonna 30c, Urtica Urens 1m
MOTION SICKNESS	Cocculus 6c, Petroleum 6c
PATELLAR LUXATION	Gelsemium Sempervirens 6c, Rhus Toxicodendron 6c
PENIS PROBLEMS	Aconitum Napellus 30c, Hepar Sulphuris Calcareum 30c, Pulsatilla 30c, Thuja Occidentalis 6c
PUPPY TEETHING	Calcarea Carbonica 6c, Chamomilla 6c, Phytolacca 6c

CDS: COGNITIVE DYSFUNCTION SYNDROME
"Old-Dog Syndrome"

There are many ways to evaluate old-dog syndrome. Veterinarians have defined CDS (cognitive dysfunction syndrome) as the gradual deterioration of cognitive abilities. These are indicated by changes in the dog's behavior. When a dog changes his routine response, and maladies have been eliminated as the cause of these behavioral changes, then CDS is the usual diagnosis.

More than half the dogs over eight years old suffer some form of CDS. The older the dog, the more chance he has of suffering from CDS. In humans, doctors often dismiss the CDS behavioral changes as part of "winding down."

There are four major signs of CDS: frequent potty accidents inside the home, sleeping much more or much less than normal, acting confused and failing to respond to social stimuli.

SYMPTOMS OF CDS

FREQUENT POTTY ACCIDENTS
- *Urinates in the house.*
- *Defecates in the house.*
- *Doesn't signal that he wants to go out.*

SLEEP PATTERNS
- *Moves much more slowly.*
- *Sleeps more than normal during the day.*
- *Sleeps less during the night.*

CONFUSION
- *Walks around listlessly and without a destination goal.*
- *Goes outside and just stands there.*
- *Appears confused with a faraway look in his eyes.*
- *Hides more often.*
- *Doesn't recognize friends.*
- *Doesn't come when called.*

FAILURE TO RESPOND TO SOCIAL STIMULI
- *Comes to people less frequently, whether called or not.*
- *Doesn't tolerate petting for more than a short time.*
- *Doesn't come to the door when you return home from work.*

Dogue de Bordeaux

The term *old* is a qualitative term. For dogs, as well as their masters, old is relative. Certainly we can all distinguish between a puppy Dogue de Bordeaux and an adult Dogue de Bordeaux—there are the obvious physical traits such as size, appearance and facial expression, as well as personality traits. Puppies and young dogs like to play with children. Children's natural exuberance is a good match for the seemingly endless energy of young dogs who like to run, jump, chase and retrieve. When dogs grow up and cease their interaction with children, they are often thought of as being too old to play with the kids. On the other hand, if a Dogue de Bordeaux is only exposed to people with quieter lifestyles, his life will normally be less active and the decrease in his activity level as he ages will not be as obvious.

If people live to be 100 years old, dogs live to be 20 years old. While this may sound a good rule of thumb, it is *very* inaccurate. When trying to compare dog years to human years, you cannot make a generalization about all dogs. You can make the generalization that 10 years is a good lifespan for a Dogue de Bordeaux, but you cannot compare it to that of a Chihuahua, for example, as many small breeds typically live longer than large breeds. Dogs are generally considered mature within three years, but they can reproduce even earlier. We can generalize to say that the first three years of a dog's life are more like seven times that of comparable humans, meaning that a 3-year-old dog is like a 21-year-old person. However, there is no hard and fast rule for comparing dog and human ages. The comparison is made even more difficult, for not all humans age at the same rate...and human females live longer than human males.

GETTING OLD

The bottom line is simply that your dog is getting old when you think he is getting old because he slows down in his level of general activity, including walking, running, eating, jumping and retrieving. On the other hand, the frequency of certain activities increases, such as more sleeping, more barking and more repetition of habits like going to the door without being called when you put your coat on to leave the house.

WHEN YOUR DOG GETS OLD...
SIGNS THE OWNER CAN LOOK FOR

IF YOU NOTICE...	IT COULD INDICATE...
Discoloration of teeth and gums, foul breath, loss of appetite	Abcesses, gum disease, mouth lesions
Lumps, bumps, cysts, warts, fatty tumors	Cancers, benign or malignant
Cloudiness of eyes, apparent loss of sight	Cataracts, lenticular sclerosis, PRA, retinal dysplasia, blindness
Flaky coat, alopecia (hair loss)	Hormonal problems, hypothyroidism
Obesity, appetite loss, excessive weight gain	Various problems
Household accidents, increased urination	Diabetes, kidney or bladder disease
Increased thirst	Kidney disease, diabetes mellitus, bladder infection
Change in sleeping habits, coughing	Heart disease
Difficulty moving	Arthritis, degenerative joint disease, spondylosis (degenerative spine disease)

ALERT YOUR VET IF YOU NOTICE THESE SYMPTOMS IN YOUR DOG!

WHAT TO LOOK FOR IN SENIORS

Most veterinarians and behaviorists use the seven-year mark as the time to consider a dog a senior. The term *senior* does not imply that the dog is geriatric and has begun to fail in mind and body. Aging is essentially a slowing process. Humans readily admit that they feel a difference in their activity level from age 20 to 30, and then from 30 to 40, etc. By treating the seven-year-old dog as a senior, owners are able to implement certain therapeutic and preventative medical strategies with the help of their

SENIOR SIGNS

An old dog starts to show one or more of the following symptoms:
- The hair on the face and paws starts to turn gray. The color breakdown usually starts around the eyes and mouth.
- Sleep patterns are deeper and longer, and the old dog is harder to awaken.
- Food intake diminishes.
- Responses to calls, whistles and other signals are ignored more and more.
- Eye contact does not evoke tail wagging (assuming it once did).

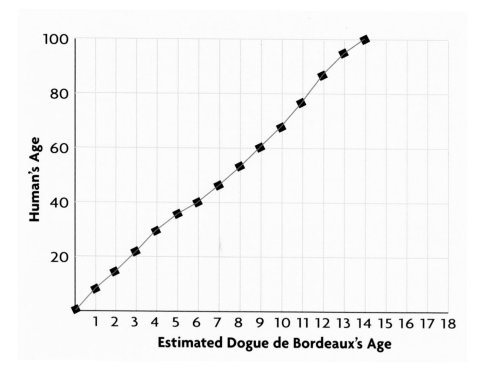

Human's Age vs. Estimated Dogue de Bordeaux's Age

veterinarians. A senior-care program should include at least two veterinary visits per year, and screening sessions to determine the dog's health status, as well as nutritional counseling. Veterinarians determine the senior dog's health status through a blood smear for a complete blood count, serum chemistry profile with electrolytes, urinalysis, blood pressure check, electrocardiogram, ocular tonometry (pressure on the eyeball) and dental prophylaxis.

Such an extensive program for senior dogs is well advised before owners start to see the obvious physical signs of aging, such as slower and inhibited movement, graying, increased sleep/nap periods and disinterest in play and other activity. This preventative program promises a longer, healthier life for the aging dog. Among the physical problems common in aging dogs are the loss of sight and hearing, arthritis, kidney and liver failure, diabetes mellitus, heart disease and Cushing's disease (a hormonal disease).

In addition to the physical manifestations discussed, there are some behavioral changes and problems related to aging dogs. Dogs suffering from hearing or vision loss, dental discomfort or arthritis can become aggressive. Likewise, the near-deaf and/or blind dog may be startled more easily and react in an unexpectedly aggressive manner. Seniors suffering from senility can become more impatient and irritable. Housesoiling accidents are associated with loss of mobility, kidney problems and loss of sphincter control as well as plaque accumulation, physiological brain changes and reactions to medications. Older dogs, just like young puppies, suffer from

NOTICING THE SYMPTOMS

The symptoms listed below are symptoms that gradually appear and become more noticeable. They are not life-threatening; however, the symptoms below are to be taken very seriously and warrant a discussion with your veterinarian:

- Your dog cries and whimpers when he moves, and he stops running completely.
- Convulsions start or become more serious and frequent. The usual convulsion (spasm) is when the dog stiffens and starts to tremble, being unable or unwilling to move. The seizure usually lasts for 5 to 30 minutes.
- Your dog drinks more water and urinates more frequently. Wetting and bowel accidents take place indoors without warning.
- Vomiting becomes more and more frequent.

separation anxiety, which can lead to excessive barking, whining, house-soiling and destructive behavior. Seniors may become fearful of everyday sounds, such as vacuum cleaners, heaters, thunder and passing traffic. Some dogs have difficulty sleeping, due to discomfort, the need for frequent potty visits and the like.

Owners should avoid spoiling the older dog with too many treats. Obesity is a common problem in older dogs and subtracts years from their lives. Keep the senior dog as trim as possible, since excess weight puts additional stress on the body's vital organs. Some breeders recommend supplementing the diet with foods high in fiber and lower in calories. Adding fresh vegetables and marrow broth to the senior's diet makes a tasty, low-calorie, low-fat supplement. Vets also offer specialty diets for senior dogs that are worth exploring.

Your dog, as he nears his twilight years, needs his owner's patience and good care more than ever. Never punish an older dog for an accident or abnormal behavior. For all the years of love, protection and companionship that your dog has provided, he deserves special attention and courtesies. The older dog may need to relieve himself at 3 a.m. because he can no longer hold it for eight hours. Older dogs may

not be able to remain crated for more than two or three hours. It may be time to give up a sofa or chair to your old friend. Although he may not seem as enthusiastic about your attention and petting, he does appreciate the considerations you offer as he gets older.

Your Dogue de Bordeaux does not understand why his world is slowing down. Owners must make their dogs' transition into the golden years as pleasant and rewarding as possible.

WHAT TO DO WHEN THE TIME COMES

You are never fully prepared to make a rational decision about putting your dog to sleep. It is very obvious that you love your Dogue de Bordeaux or you would not be reading this book. Putting a loved dog to sleep is extremely difficult. It is a decision that must be made with your veterinarian. You are usually forced to make the decision when your dog experiences one or more life-threaten-

AGING ADDITIVES

A healthy diet is important for dogs of all ages, but older dogs may benefit from the addition of supplements like antioxidants, which fight the aging process, and vitamin B, which aids the kidneys. Check with your vet before adding these or any supplements to your pet's diet.

Your veterinarian usually can assist you in locating a pet cemetery in which you can memorialize your dog.

ing symptoms, requiring you to seek veterinary help.

If the prognosis of the malady indicates the end is near and your beloved pet will only suffer more and experience no enjoyment for the balance of his life, then euthanasia is the right choice.

What is Euthanasia?

Euthanasia derives from the Greek, meaning *good death*. It means the planned, painless killing of a dog suffering from a painful, incurable condition, or who is so aged that he cannot walk, see, eat or control his excretory functions.

Euthanasia is usually accomplished by injection with an overdose of an anesthesia or barbitu-

rate. Aside from the prick of the needle, the experience is usually painless.

Making the Decision

The days during which the dog becomes ill and the end occurs can be unusually stressful for you. Usually your dog can be maintained on drugs for a few days while he is kept in the vet's clinic in order to give you ample time to make a decision. If you are the head of the family and have children, you should involve them in the decision of putting your Dogue de Bordeaux to sleep. Both the decision-making process and euthanasia itself are painful and stressful for the family of the dog.

There are facilities at most pet cemeteries in which you can keep your pet's ashes after cremation.

If this is your first experience with the death of a loved one, you may need the comfort dictated by your religious beliefs. Talking with members of the family or people who have lived through this same experience can ease the burden of your inevitable and difficult decision.

THE FINAL RESTING PLACE

Dogs can have some of the same privileges as humans. They can be buried in a pet cemetery, which is generally expensive, or, if they have died at home, can be buried in the owner's yard in a place suitably marked with some stone or a newly planted tree or bush. Alternatively, dogs can be cremated and the ashes returned to their owners, or some people prefer to leave their dogs at the vet's clinic.

All of these options should be discussed frankly and openly with your veterinarian. Do not be afraid to ask financial questions.

For example, cremations can be individual, but a less expensive option is mass cremation, although of course the ashes of individual dogs cannot then be returned. Vets can usually arrange cremation services on your behalf, or help you locate a nearby pet cemetery.

GETTING ANOTHER DOG?

The grief of losing your beloved dog will be as lasting as the grief of losing a human friend or relative. In most cases, if your dog died of old age (if there is such a thing), he had slowed down considerably. Do you want a new Dogue de Bordeaux puppy? Perhaps you would prefer a different breed to avoid comparison with your old friend.

Most people usually stay with the same breed because they know and love the characteristics of that breed. Then, too, they often know people who have the same breed and perhaps they are lucky enough that a breeder whom they know and respect expects a litter soon. What could be better?

TALK IT OUT

The more openly your family discusses the whole stressful occurrence of the aging and eventual loss of a beloved pet, the easier it will be for you when the time comes.

When you purchase your Dogue de Bordeaux, you will make it clear to the breeder whether you want one just as a devoted companion and pet, or if you hope to be buying a Dogue de Bordeaux with show prospects. No reputable breeder will sell you a young puppy and tell you that it is *definitely* of show quality, for so much can go wrong during the early months of a puppy's development. If you plan to show, what you will hopefully have acquired is a puppy with "show potential."

To the novice, exhibiting a Dogue de Bordeaux in the show ring may look easy, but it takes a lot of hard work and devotion to do top winning at a show such as the ARBA Cherry Blossom Show or the World Dog Show, not to mention a little luck too!

The first concept that the canine novice learns when watching a dog show is that each dog first competes against members of his own breed. Once the judge has selected the best member of each breed (Best of Breed), provided that the show is judged on a Group system, that chosen dog will compete with other dogs in his group. Finally, the dogs chosen first in each group will compete for Best in Show.

The second concept that you must understand is that the dogs are not actually compared against one another. The judge compares each dog against his breed standard, the written description of the ideal specimen that is approved by the Fédération Cynologique Internationale (FCI). While some early breed standards were indeed based on specific dogs that were

CLUB CONTACTS
You can get information about dog shows from kennel clubs and breed clubs:

Fédération Cynologique Internationale
14, rue Leopold II, B-6530 Thuin, Belgium
www.fci.be

American Rare Breed Association
9921 Frank Tippett Road
Cheltenham, MD 20623
www.arba.org

United Kennel Club
100 E. Kilgore Road
Kalamazoo, MI 49002
www.ukcdogs.com

The Kennel Club
1-5 Clarges St.,
Piccadilly, London W1Y 8AB, UK
www.the-kennel-club.org.uk

famous or popular, many dedicated enthusiasts say that a perfect specimen, as described in the standard, has never walked into a show ring, has never been bred and, to the woe of dog breeders around the globe, does not exist. Breeders attempt to get as close to this ideal as possible with every litter, but theoretically the "perfect" dog is so elusive that it is impossible. (And if the "perfect" dog were born, breeders and judges would never agree that it was indeed "perfect.")

If you are interested in exploring the world of dog showing, your best bet is to join your local breed club or a national club like the Dogue de Bordeaux Society or United States Bordeaux

Corporation. These clubs often host both regional and national specialties, shows only for Dogues de Bordeaux, which can include conformation as well as obedience and agility trials. Even if you have no intention of competing with your Dogue de Bordeaux, a specialty is like a festival for lovers of the breed who congregate to share their favorite topic: Dogues! Clubs also send out newsletters, and some organize training days and seminars in order that people may learn more about their chosen breed. To locate the breed club closest to you, contact the American Rare Breed Association (ARBA), which furnishes the rules and regulations for many events for the

The Dogue de Bordeaux makes quite a giant impression in the show ring, especially when as majestically constructed as this international champion.

Dogues de Bordeaux in the breed ring. The judge compares the dogs not to each other, but rather to the requirements detailed in the breed standard.

breed and other rare breeds, or the United Kennel Club.

If your Dogue de Bordeaux is six months of age or older and registered with the sponsoring club, you can enter him in a dog show where the breed is offered classes. Provided that your Dogue de Bordeaux does not have a disqualifying fault, he can compete. Only unaltered dogs can be entered in a dog show, so if you have spayed or neutered your Dogue de Bordeaux, your dog cannot compete in conformation shows. The reason for this is simple. Dog shows are the main forum to prove which representatives of a breed are worthy of being bred. Only dogs that have achieved championships—the dog world's "seal of approval" for quality in pure-bred dogs—-

should be bred. Altered dogs, however, can participate in other events, such as obedience trials.

Before you actually step into the ring, you would be well advised to sit back and observe the judge's ring procedure. If it is your first time in the ring, do not be over-anxious and run to the front of the line. It is much better to stand back and study how the exhibitor in front of you is performing. The judge asks each handler to "stack" the dog, hopefully showing the dog off to his best advantage. The judge will observe the dog from a distance and from different angles, and approach the dog to check his teeth, overall structure, alertness and muscle tone, as well as consider how well the dog "conforms" to the standard. Most importantly, the judge will have the exhibitor move the dog around the ring in some pattern that he should specify. Finally, the judge will give the dog one last look before moving on to the next exhibitor.

If you are not in the top four in your class at your first show, do not be discouraged. Be patient and consistent, and you may eventually find yourself in a winning line-up. Remember that the winners were once in your shoes and have devoted many hours and much money to earn the placement. If you find that your dog is losing every time and never getting a nod, it may be time to consider a different dog sport or to just enjoy your Dogue de Bordeaux as a pet. Parent clubs offer other events, such as agility, tracking, obedience, instinct tests and more, which may be of interest to the owner of a well-trained Dogue de Bordeaux.

FÉDÉRATION CYNOLOGIQUE INTERNATIONALE

Established in 1911, the Fédération Cynologique Internationale (FCI) represents the "world kennel club." This international body brings uniformity to the breeding, judging and showing of pure-bred dogs. Although the FCI originally included only five European nations: France, Germany, Austria, the Netherlands and Belgium (which remains its head-quarters), the organization today embraces nations on six continents and recognizes well over 300 breeds of pure-bred dog. There are three titles attainable through the FCI: the International Champion, which is the most prestigious; the International Beauty Champion, which is based on aptitude certificates in different countries; and the International Trial Champion, which is based on achievement in obedience trials in different countries. The FCI sponsors both national and international shows. The hosting country determines

SHOW-RING ETIQUETTE

Just as with anything else, there is a certain etiquette to the show ring that can only be learned through experience. Showing your dog can be quite intimidating to you as a novice when it seems as if everyone else knows what he is doing. You can familiarize yourself with ring procedure beforehand by taking showing classes to prepare you and your dog for conformation showing and by talking with experienced handlers. When you are in the ring, it is very important to pay attention and listen to the instructions you are given by the judge about where to move your dog. Remember, even the most skilled handlers had to start somewhere. Keep it up and you too will become a proficient handler as you gain practice and experience.

The judge examines carefully and pays close attention to the unique head and undershot bite of the Dogue de Bordeaux. Precise specifications are set forth for the Dogue's undershot bite—the lower jaw must extend beyond the upper jaw by 0.5 to 2.0 cm, which is approximately .2 to .8 in.

the judging system and breed standards are always based on the breed's country of origin. Dogs from every country can participate in these impressive canine spectacles, the largest of which is the World Dog Show, hosted in a different country each year.

The FCI is divided into 10 Groups, and the Dogue de Bordeaux competes in Group 2 with the Molossoids. At the World Dog Show, the following classes are offered for each breed: Puppy Class (6–9 months), Junior Class (9–18 months), Open Class (15 months or older) and Champion Class. A dog can be awarded a classification of Excellent, Very Good, Good, Sufficient and Not Sufficient. Puppies can be awarded classifications of Very Promising, Promising or Not Promising. Four placements are made in each class. After all classes are judged, a Best of Breed is selected. Other special groups and classes may also be shown. Each exhibitor showing a dog receives a written evaluation from the judge.

Besides the World Dog Show and the European Champions Show, you can exhibit your dog at specialty shows held by different breed clubs. Specialty shows may have their own regulations.

My Dogue de Bordeaux

PUT YOUR PUPPY'S FIRST PICTURE HERE

Dog's Name _____

Date _____ Photographer _____